Providence *in the* Story of Scripture

The Work of God through Creation, Fall, Redemption, and New Creation

Adamson Co

a division of Baker Publishing Group
Grand Rapids, Michigan

Published by Baker Academic
a division of Baker Publishing Group
Grand Rapids, Michigan
BakerAcademic.com

Printed in the United States of America

Library of Congress Cataloging-in-Publication Data
Names: Co, Adamson, 1964– author.
Title: Providence in the story of Scripture : the work of God through creation, fall, redemption, and new creation / Adamson Co.
Description: Grand Rapids, Michigan : Baker Academic, a division of Baker Publishing Group, [2025] | Includes bibliographical references and index.
Identifiers: LCCN 2024037758 | ISBN 9781540965455 (paperback) | ISBN 9781540966742 (casebound) | ISBN 9781493442584 (ebook) | ISBN 9781493442591 (pdf)
Subjects: LCSH: Providence and government of God—Biblical teaching.
Classification: LCC BS544 .C625 2025 | DDC 231—dc23/eng/20241001
LC record available at https://lccn.loc.gov/2024037758

Any italics in Scripture have been added by the author for emphasis.

Cover image: Pictures from History / Universal Images

Baker Publishing Group publications use paper produced from sustainable forestry practices and postconsumer waste whenever possible.

25 26 27 28 29 30 31 7 6 5 4 3 2 1

To my beloved, Wensley, and the four Co boys:
Aiden, Aldridge, Avery, and Allister—

May you inhabit and anticipate God's providence
of the eighth day of creation
even as you live and bask in the providence
of his seventh day of creation

Contents

Foreword

Kevin J. Vanhoozer

The television sitcom *Father Knows Best* went off the air decades ago, not least because the show's title became increasingly implausible. Similarly, the idea that "our Father who art in heaven" knows best is one that people today struggle to take seriously, not only because of the perennial problem of evil but also because of recent history, including two world wars and a flu that killed more people than did the combined world wars. Too many people continue to experience unjust suffering, hunger, and hardship on a daily basis. Is God there, and if so, does he care?

In 1952, G. C. Berkouwer began his monograph on the doctrine of providence with a chapter entitled "The Crisis of the Providence Doctrine in Our Century." The poet W. H. Auden described the twentieth century as an "age of anxiety," and the twenty-first century has only exacerbated the situation.[1] The crisis has to do with making the reality of God meaningful in and to a secularized world acutely aware of the meaninglessness of matter in motion—the only reality many think is plausible given the rise of modern science and scientific rationality. Despite the enormity of the challenge, Berkouwer concludes his chapter on the crisis of providence by saying "the Church must not lose her courage, nor the strength of her

1. W. H. Auden, *The Age of Anxiety: A Baroque Eclogue* (New York: Random House, 1947).

witness."[2] Yet it is precisely the courage and strength of the church's witness that the present situation has put into question.

Is it only a coincidence that the crisis in the doctrine of providence overlaps with what the Korean-German philosopher Byung-Chul Han has identified as the crisis of narration? What gives rise to this latter crisis is the late-modern awareness that our stories are constructed, man-made rather than God-given. Whereas T. S. Eliot mourned the loss of wisdom in knowledge and the loss of knowledge in information, Han mourns the loss of narration in a surfeit of information: "In the post-narrative era, the calendar is de-narrativized; it becomes a meaningless schedule of appointments."[3]

In spite of secularism, science, and suffering, one still hears people claim that "everything happens for a reason." The statement can reflect anything from a belief in karma (where the universe somehow achieves moral balance) or fatalistic determinism to wishful thinking or coping mechanisms. In any case, it is a claim without a context, a bald assertion without a broader narrative that can explain away the sheer contingency of what is actually happening.

Adamson Co has written this book in response to both crises: of providence and of narration. The theologically correct version of the claim that "everything happens for a reason" is "God causes all things to work together for good to those who love God" (Rom. 8:28). Paul's claim is part of the larger biblical narrative—what for Christians is the true story of the world—that Co retrieves in order to recover the sense that there is meaning in what, apart from the biblical narrative, appears to be but chance and chaos. In the creation narrative, God asks Adam, "Where are you?" (Gen. 3:9). If the creation narrative is to orient us, then Co thinks we also need to ask, "*When* are you?" Clearly, we haven't yet achieved the rest for which Augustine says our hearts constantly yearn. When, then, in the story of creation are we?

Co rightly sees that what people take as the true story of the world is the operating system that runs their lives. Many people, having accepted the story of modern science, believe we are inhabiting a physical world only, a realm of nature with no room for the supernatural. It is as though

2. G. C. Berkouwer, *The Providence of God* (Grand Rapids: Eerdmans, 1952), 29.

3. Byung-Chul Han, *The Crisis of Narration*, trans. Daniel Steuer (Cambridge: Polity, 2024), viii.

we are living in the cosmos whose creation is depicted in the first six days of creation only. The story of Genesis does not stop there, however. If it did, it would give rise to a deistic picture, according to which God creates and then withdraws from his creation, leaving nature to its own devices (i.e., natural laws). Deism affirms the existence of God, but its God is not personally involved in, and thus in loving relationship with, the world. The deist doctrine of providence asserts only that God has set up the initial conditions for the smooth running of the cosmos. However, in the event that something goes wrong to disturb the created order, deists do not expect God to intervene and put things right. The deist God does not make house calls.

Providence in the Story of Scripture is properly theistic, indeed trinitarian, not deistic. Co takes his cue from church fathers who viewed the Lord's Day not simply as the seventh day of Sabbath rest but rather as the eighth day of creation: the first day of the new creation, the beginning of the end of the story that concludes with heaven, God's kingdom, coming down to earth (or earth being caught up to heaven).

According to the biblical story, Christians live not simply in the natural world created in the first six days but in a world that is in the process of being redeemed, a world that exists in the time in between Jesus's first and second comings. All this to say, the triune God is on the move, in love reaching out to the world with his two hands, Son and Spirit. In the words of the apostle Paul: "Therefore if anyone is in Christ, this person is a new creation; the old things passed away; behold, new things have come" (2 Cor. 5:17).

Co is well aware of the crisis of providence. However, he has chosen to write not an ABC primer on the doctrine but, even better, a *picture* book. The aim is not to formulate new answers to age-old conundrums: that way *academic* theology lies. Co instead addresses the *pastoral* problem of how to once again make the doctrine of providence a lively belief—a teaching that comes alive and actually affects our day-to-day existence, providing hope, meaning, and purpose. In focusing on the biblical story rather than philosophical arguments, Co keeps company with other contemporary thinkers, such as Eleonore Stump, who argue that some problems are best approached not through technical formulations or conceptual elaborations but through narratives.[4] The narrative picture of eighth-day creation retrieves the idea that our Father in heaven *does* know best even if we have to wait and trust him for the happy ending, thereby changing the metaphor or story we live by. Calvin knew that one of the purposes of the doctrine of providence was to provide believers with the resilience to endure "the sufferings of this present time" (Rom. 8:18), knowing that the ending of the story will be altogether glorious.

The moral of the story: "Today is the first day of the eighth day of creation." Today, the *eighth* day, is the day Christians must seize, and live, to God's glory. When the church lives out the already/not-yet eighth day of creation, thus reframing divine providence, it becomes a parable of God's kingdom—what Co memorably calls "the world's Tomorrowland"—namely, a glimpse into creation's future.

Providence in the Story of Scripture is a wake-up call to those of us who have lost hope because we no longer have a compelling narrative by which to make sense of things. Where in the world are we? In whose story? The biblical story is the true (because divinely revealed) account of God, the world, and ourselves. Co reminds us, however, that we are not there yet, at story's end. His purpose is not to solve an intellectual riddle but to provide a pastoral aid to making the doctrine of divine providence existentially relevant. As he says in the book, we can only live into the story of God's fatherly care if we "reboot" our theological imaginations. This is precisely his purpose: to retrieve the biblical story, and the eighth day of creation, as a crucial means for training us to *see*, *taste,* and *experience* the world "in process," already but not yet fully made gloriously new in Christ.

4. See Eleonore Stump, *Wandering in Darkness: Narrative and the Problem of Suffering* (Oxford: Clarendon, 2010), 23–82.

Acknowledgments

The task of writing a book is akin to taking a long journey. The path to its completion is fraught with many unexpected challenges that could easily derail the trip at any point in its development. The fact that this journey has reached its final destination in the form of this completed book is a testament to God's good hand of providence at work all throughout the process, for which I am deeply humbled and grateful. It is to the furtherance of his kingdom purposes that this book is written. May the triune God of the Bible be pleased and glorified!

The Lord has providentially used many individuals along the way, and I wish to and must express my gratitude. During the book's initial phase, I approached many in the theological community for their input on its basic thesis and thrust. They have been most gracious to give me their time to interact with me despite their busy schedules. Their advice and words of encouragement have served as the impetus for the beginning of this book project. These early consultants included Kevin Vanhoozer, Robert Yarbrough, Dan Treier, Fred Sanders, and Dave Nelson, my former editor at Baker Academic. Their confidence in the feasibility of the book project meant so much to me, especially in the grind of the writing process. I hope that the final product does justice to their initial confidence in the project.

Within the academic community, I am thankful for my colleagues at California Baptist University for those moments when I could just drop by their offices to exchange ideas on my book as well as other theological issues. I am especially appreciative of the scholarly example and advice that my dean, Chris Morgan, has given me and my colleagues on what it means to be engaged in theological scholarship in the service of the church and its work. This book certainly is aligned with that vision.

The entire Baker Academic staff has been very supportive from the beginning to the end of the writing process. I am grateful to have patient editors in the persons of Anna Gissing and Eric Salo, who gave me wise counsel along the way. Thank you.

While I was writing, the church that I formerly pastored, Mandarin Baptist Church of Los Angeles, approached me to serve as their interim pastor. It was a joy not only to get reacquainted with them again after being away for so many years but also to share with them many of the teachings found in this book. My adult Sunday school class during that time attentively listened to me share the ideas of the book and graciously interacted and engaged with me with their thoughts. In this way, they have made the book so much better and more accessible. Inasmuch as I have sought to bless them with pastoral teaching and care, they have actually blessed me with their honest responses to the book's ideas. What a great adult Sunday school class I had. May their tribe increase!

Finally, writing a book cannot help but be a family affair. How could it be otherwise? I had to spend so much time with the project that everyone in the family had no choice but to come to know this "stranger" in our midst—directly or indirectly. By the time the book was done, this "stranger" had become part of our family. My siblings and their spouses have even given me invaluable advice on how best to introduce and present the book to someone outside the family. Their tips were most helpful.

For two years or so, my wife and four sons patiently allowed me to spend extra time on the writing of this book. Thankfully, not only did they endure the occasional intrusion of this "stranger" into our family time, but also they have come to know and appreciate this project for themselves even as they took part in supporting it in their own way—each one doing what they could, no matter how menial, in order to see the book's final completion. I am grateful for the love of my family that sustained me during that long process. Additionally, I marvel at how their unique participation has transformed this personal writing task into a kind of family project. Looking back now at the end of this long writing journey, I cannot help but cherish the enduring imagery of our family's blended effort toward a common goal. For that very special memory, I shall always be thankful to them and to the Lord.

Preface

A Seventh and Eighth Days of Creation Narrative Approach

> And Jesus said to them, "Therefore every scribe who has become a disciple of the kingdom of heaven is like a head of a household, who brings out of his treasure new things and old."
>
> —Matthew 13:52

The traditional way of teaching the doctrine of providence in systematic theology is to discuss the elements of preservation, governance, and also in many instances, concurrence. It then goes on to deal with the issue of divine sovereignty and human free will. Additionally, it addresses the thorny issue of the problem of evil. While these are tried-and-true approaches to teaching providence, for some students they are too abstract or complex and even detached from real-life situations. This is especially true for the introductory students I envision using this book.

I emphasize that my approach here is not a departure from more traditional ways of teaching the doctrine of providence but is complementary and supplementary to them. In fact, this book includes an overview of the doctrine of providence in that traditional manner so as to inform students of what the doctrine teaches. But, after that, to bolster and deepen their appreciation of the doctrine of providence, I present my own approach based on the seventh and eighth days of creation. My approach is an attempt to introduce a *narrative dimension* to the doctrine of providence.

In the study of Christian theology today much emphasis is placed on the six days of creation. Our preoccupation with that particular issue, however, may blind us to an even more important topic of theological discussion: the seventh day and the much-anticipated eighth day of creation. These neglected "days of creation" are actually, in my view, some of the choice marrow of Christian theology. For in them, not only is God's power to create affirmed, but also his gracious purposes and provision for creaturely existence are demonstrated and are shown to satisfy the human soul. In short, the seventh and eighth days of creation pave the way for our existential understanding and practical living out of God's reasons in creating us.

The motif of the "seventh and eighth days of creation" is not novel to this book but traces its origin back to the ancient church. Early Christian theologians such as Justin Martyr, Cyprian, Basil, and Augustine, to name but a few, used this creation motif to do theology. In particular, they used the "seventh and eighth days of creation" as a heuristic device to highlight God's loving provision for humanity found in Christ's work of redemption and new creation.[1] Vestiges of this ancient approach can still be seen today in the church's day of worship established on Sunday instead of on Saturday. Over time, the motif fell into disuse. That is why we do not hear much about it these days. In light of this motif's decline, this book serves as a reappropriation of an ancient theological theme now applied in the context of the doctrine of providence.

I propose to use the "seventh and eighth days of creation" as a theological framework to help bring clarity to the doctrine of providence by setting the parameter of the discourse within that biblical motif, thus avoiding unnecessary complexity while at the same time maintaining theological precision. In this book I aim to show that the seventh day (biblical history's thrust toward "redemption") and the eighth day (biblical history's thrust toward "new creation") of creation are theological "lenses" that facilitate our understanding and the application of the Bible's teaching on providence in relation to human existence.

This book, then, utilizes the creation motif of the Bible to provide a "picturesque" introductory guide to the biblical doctrine of providence. It

1. See Vos and Wainright, *Liturgical Time*.

deliberately incorporates, where appropriate, discussions of key doctrines of Christianity in order to present the "big picture" of Christian theology in relation to the doctrine of providence. In short, it preserves the Bible's metanarrative of creation, fall, redemption, and new creation, even while it explicates the doctrine of providence in an overview fashion.

Introduction

Recapturing the Biblical Imagination

> The king [Nebuchadnezzar] answered Daniel and said, "Surely your God is a God of gods and a Lord of kings and a revealer of mysteries, since you have been able to reveal this mystery."
>
> —Daniel 2:47

God is never more fully appreciated as "God" than when the human heart truly comprehends the doctrine of providence. For providence conveys the soul-nurturing truth that God not only created us but also graciously provides for all of our human needs and guides us along throughout our human existence. So, it should be one of the most cherished and useful doctrines in Christian theology. Sadly, it's not. Many reasons can be given for this phenomenon, but here we limit ourselves to two.

First, we live in an era influenced by what philosopher Charles Taylor calls "the immanent frame." To introduce this concept, Taylor asks the provocative question, "Why was it virtually impossible not to believe in God in, say, 1500 in our Western society, while in 2000 many of us find this not only easy, but even inescapable?"[1] The answer: modern humanity is living in an "immanent frame"—that is, a lens or a framework of viewing life as "taking place within a self-sufficient immanent order."[2] Alister McGrath, a scholar of science and religion, says that it is "a view

1. Taylor, *A Secular Age*, 25.
2. Taylor, *A Secular Age*, 543.

of human flourishing which denies or suppresses any notion of a transcendent source of morality . . . and which refuses to recognize any good beyond this life and world (also known as exclusive humanism)."[3] The "immanent frame" forms the basis of our present "secular age."[4] So when it comes to the doctrine of providence whereby humanity is seen as dependent upon the providential care and guidance of a Transcendent Being, it is no wonder that the concept does not resonate today. But, as Taylor describes it, humans embrace this "immanent frame" of thinking to their own detriment.

Unfortunately, this "immanent frame" of thinking and living is not limited to those outside Christianity. Fifty years ago, J. I. Packer wrote in his classic book *Knowing God* this diagnosis on the theological condition then, which is true also of our present time:

> It is often said today that theology is stronger than it has ever been, and in terms of academic expertise and the quantity and quality of books published this is probably true; but it is a long time since theology has been so weak and clumsy at its basic task of holding the church to the realities of the gospel.[5]

The reason Packer gave for Christian theology's inability to fully communicate its rich truths is the strong countervailing influence of "modern skepticism" that has crept into the Christian community and, in turn, created an attitude of "uncertainty and confusion about God."[6]

The second reason why the doctrine of providence is poorly appreciated today is that the doctrine is mired in abstraction and controversy. Thus, it is often relegated to the dustbin of cold academic discussions. Here, the posture taken by many Christian theologians on the subject of providence has not helped the cause of promoting a clear understanding of the doctrine. In the minds of many people, the doctrine of providence is too complex, reserved only for the theological elites.[7] Since most people do

3. McGrath, "Hesitations about Special Divine Action," 8.

4. See also Smith, *How (Not) to Be Secular*.

5. Packer, *Knowing God*, 7.

6. Packer, *Knowing God*, 6–7.

7. Due to the doctrine's complexity, Roger Olson goes on to make this claim: "This has become one of the most divisive issues within Protestant Christian circles." Olson, *Mosaic of Christian Belief*, 179.

not fall into the highbrow category, they quickly lose interest in the subject of providence. So instead of impressing the importance of providence for today's society, exponents of this view inadvertently create the opposite effect through the way they communicate the doctrine.

Can anything be done to address the situation? This book takes the affirmative view. But how? Citing C. S. Lewis, Alister McGrath helpfully notes that the "immanent frame" we live in is like a spell that has mesmerized us. To break it, we will need a stronger spell. What this means practically is that "Christianity has to show that it can tell a more compelling and engaging story that will capture the imagination of its culture."[8] And the way to break this spell is "not by rational argument, but by capturing the cultural imagination with a richer and deeper vision of reality."[9]

Taking Lewis and McGrath's narrative cue, this book advocates a "creational frame" to help break the "immanent frame" so prevalent in our society when thinking about God and, in particular, when thinking about the doctrine of providence. Specifically, I propose a theological framework for looking at providence and human existence that is grounded on the Bible's motif of the seventh and eighth days of creation. Such an approach addresses in a constructive way the problems raised in our secular age, for it informs us what the biblical view is in a simple, straightforward manner. And, at the same time, it also stimulates our imaginations to dig deeper into how God engages us in the world for the purpose of living in that reality.

Above and beyond addressing the impediment of secularity in one's grasp of providence, this way of framing our understanding of God and his providence is actually a retrieval of an ancient Christian approach to doing theology. It taps into the rich resources of those who came before us whom the Holy Spirit has also instructed for our benefit today.

Another term for Sunday or the Lord's Day is the "eighth day" of creation. The "eighth day" is a phrase coined by the early church fathers to designate both the day when Christ rose from the dead (first day of a new week, therefore, the eighth day) and the new era that Christ ushered in through his resurrection from the dead (the beginning of God's work of re-creation for the benefit of humanity, a day when he resumed his work of

8. McGrath, "Hesitations about Special Divine Action," 6.

9. McGrath, "Hesitations about Special Divine Action," 9.

creation after he "rested" on the seventh day). Eugene Fairweather explains how the rationale for this designation came about. He says that while "the phrase 'the first day of the week' speaks directly to a particular day when a particular event happened, it has symbolic overtones which Christian ears can scarcely fail to hear."[10] This is the inescapable comparison that Christians saw through their biblically informed lens of seeing reality:

> On the first day of the creation God made the light shine out of the darkness of the still formless world. On the first day of the resurrection God brought the Light of eternal life out of the darkness of the grave. As the early Christians saw it, the Light of time prefigured the Light of eternity and the Light of eternity fulfilled the promise of the Light of time. The first day of the creation saw the universe of creatures begin to emerge from God's hands; the first day of the resurrection saw created manhood raised up in glory, the first fruits of the new creation. On the first day of the creation God's transcendent purpose for man was foreshadowed; on the first day of the resurrection that same purpose was realized.[11]

Fairweather goes on to explain, "Seen in this perspective . . . the Lord's Day on the first day of the week is a sign of the inauguration of a new creation in Christ."[12] It is, thus, rightly described as the eighth day of creation because the "new creation is not simply a return to the beginning, a fresh start for the world of nature. The new creation is a new and fresh and supernatural act of the creator, which emancipates man from the natural limits of creaturely life and takes him up into eternal communion with God."[13]

With eloquence and exuberance, Fairweather captures the proper attitude that the church seeks to embody each time it gathers to worship on a Sunday—the Lord's Day, the eighth day:

> Sunday is not just a ritual occasion, let alone a day arbitrarily hedged in by quaint taboos. Sunday is one of the great historic symbols of the crucified and risen Christ. Sunday is the Lord's Day—not in any exclusive sense, as if all days did not belong to the King of ages, but because on this day the

10. Fairweather, *Meaning and Message of Lent*, 106.
11. Fairweather, *Meaning and Message of Lent*, 106.
12. Fairweather, *Meaning and Message of Lent*, 107.
13. Fairweather, *Meaning and Message of Lent*, 107.

> Lord Christ rose from death. Sunday is the Lord's Day because on this day God's purpose for mankind was accomplished in Christ. Sunday is the Lord's Day because on this day God inaugurated his new creation. Sunday is a sign of what God has done in Christ and a token of what God will do in us. Sunday is a glimpse through the gate of death—a glimpse of our final destiny in God.[14]

Thus, as believers gather on a Sunday to worship, they are not only reminded of what Christ has done for them through God's providence. They also leave their place of worship as an eighth-day community to bear witness to a world yearning for God's providential intervention, for he has indeed given us an eighth day of creation to look forward to in the future and to inhabit even now.

This book's approach, therefore, stems from the theology and practice of the early church. Given the motif's neglect over the years, we, like Isaac re-digging his father Abraham's well in Genesis (26:18), might just rediscover a methodology that can still yield theological insights to our great benefit. But, most important of all, the theological frame of the seventh and eighth days of creation is rooted thoroughly in Scripture. And for that reason, we can be assured that we are in good standing as we approach the doctrine of providence in a rather constructive and albeit less-than-typical systematic theology fashion.

The Terry Waite Predicament as Paradigm

Betrayed. Kidnapped. Isolated. That's what happened to Terry Waite while on a peace mission in Beirut, Lebanon, on behalf of the archbishop of Canterbury in 1987. Instead of brokering the release of hostages from the hands of Hezbollah, the extremist Islamic group, Waite himself became their hostage for almost five years! His captors confined him in a small cell with no windows, and he was often kept blindfolded or in complete darkness.

The shock of what happened soon developed into deep anger within him and eventually gave way to a much more necessary survival mindset. But life as a hostage, at that point, was so "disorientating" that it was

14. Fairweather, *Meaning and Message of Lent*, 107–8.

hard to maintain a normal life. He had no awareness of the time of the day or the day of the week. Waite said, "I'd wake up, perhaps at . . . I don't know what time it was. It could have been in the middle of the night, and I'd think it was the morning. And I just got completely lost."[15] So, if he was to survive, he knew that the first thing to do was for him to know the time so that he could properly order his life.

But how? How could he tell time under his claustrophobic confinement? Waite said that in certain places where he was held captive, "it was possible to get a structure to the day simply because I was kept near to a mosque. And I got the call from the minaret, morning—daybreak—noon, and dusk. And that gave me a pattern for the day. And I found it important to build a pattern for the day, so that I would put a period of time aside to think along certain lines . . . to exercise my brain, I suppose."

In an especially touching vignette, Terry Waite further tells of a practice he engaged in during captivity. Despite not being a clergyman, Waite said, "I would save a little bread from my supper, and I'd have a little water in the cup. And I would say to myself the Communion service." Then, during that personal solemn moment of communion with God, Waite said, "I'd say to myself, in saying that service . . . I was linking myself with others on the outside who were saying the same service. And I'd locate myself in my imagination—for example, in a cathedral I'd known or a parish church I'd known." But what good did that practice do for Terry Waite the hostage of Hezbollah? He said that it gave him "a sense of position and identity"—one that no captor could limit or take away. In the act of communion with God, Terry Waite was transported to a different realm, to a different dimension, to a sacred time of human existence far above his present limitations. That was how Terry Waite survived and even thrived in the years of his captivity.

More likely than not, very few of us have experienced captivity as Terry Waite did. But there are moments—perhaps more often than we care to admit—when our lives resemble Terry Waite's captivity, figuratively speaking. We are disorientated. And we don't know what to do under the circumstances. In such a case, what Terry Waite did to survive and thrive in his captivity is what we need to do as well. We too must

15. All quotations here are from "Terry Waite—Knowing Day/Time and Maintaining Routines," YouTube video, posted by Christian Doctrine, May 7, 2021, https://youtu.be/7ZxICPIlbWY.

know the time—the time of the day and, I add, the day of the week—if we are to get a proper orientation on life and know the divine provisions available for us therein. That's what the doctrine of providence is all about. One of the roles of Christian theology is to help us "tell time," making for a meaningful human existence. Such is the approach this book takes for apprehending the doctrine of providence. In knowing the time we live in—whether the seventh day or the eighth day of creation—we can better understand God's providential enablement and organize our life accordingly. The seventh and eighth days of creation provide the theological framework for us to properly appropriate and therefore benefit from God's providence according to the biblical significance of these days.

This Book's Intended Audience and Goals

This is an introductory book on providence. It is not intended to compete with or replace in-depth studies on providence. I have in mind readers who may or may not have a solid background in Christian theology. My goal is to show them the relevance of theology—providence, in particular—for their life in an engaging fashion without diluting the theological content. In short, it is written for the Terry Waite in all of us. Given the intended audience, I aim to be creatively concise in this short book.

Despite my intention, I realize that the doctrine of providence will remain, in some sense, complex. The key, however, is to not make it unnecessarily complex. To that end, this is the reason I am employing the biblical motif of the seventh and eighth days of creation throughout the book to help the readers build their theological framework for understanding providence. I believe that this approach will indeed foster in their minds and hearts the beauty of the doctrine's simplicity, clarity, and saliency, regardless of the readers' present familiarity with providence.

Further, this book takes the view that providence is best taught in the context of living out one's station in life. Thus, discussions on providence in this book emphasize its correlation to human vocation. In this way, readers should not find a moment of irrelevance about providence, since the book's treatment of the subject naturally relates to their own human existence or vocation.

Finally, beyond showing my readers the relevance of providence for their own human existence, I hope to guide them to a greater awareness of time itself and thereby develop a different way of keeping track of one's time on earth. This book, then, seeks to reorient our sense of time to a Christian understanding of it by relating our present time (human existence) to God's time or timing (providence) as demonstrated in the biblical motif of the seventh and eighth days of creation. In this way of understanding time, we come to understand in a deeper way what the doctrine of providence is truly all about.

A "Full Plan of God" Approach

John Stott makes this jolting observation of how the Christian message is often perceived and received in our society: "Many people are rejecting our gospel today, not because they perceive it to be false, but because they perceive it to be trivial. They are looking for an integrated worldview that makes sense of all their experience."[16] Stott thinks that the problem of "triviality" stems from our truncated, oversimplified approach to the Christian message. Thus, he prescribes the following: "Today's world needs a bigger gospel, the full gospel of Scripture, what Paul later in Ephesus was to call 'the entire plan of God'" (Acts 20:27).[17] Like Paul's approach to the pagan philosophers of Athens in Acts 17, "we cannot preach the gospel of Jesus without the doctrine of God, or the cross without creation, or salvation without judgment, or vice versa."[18] In our society that is fast becoming like ancient Athens, Stott's observation could not be more apropos when presenting any doctrinal matters. We need to incorporate salvation history—which contains the entire plan of God—if we are to rise above the perception of triviality. That is, indeed, the stated purpose of this book when it comes to the doctrine of providence. For in this holistic manner of presenting the doctrine of providence, it provides an integrated worldview that makes sense of all of our experience in light of providence, and, even more importantly, it beckons us to deliberately inhabit the reality of God's providence, thereby truly benefiting from it.

16. Stott, *Through the Bible*, 334.
17. Stott, *Through the Bible*, 334.
18. Stott, *Through the Bible*, 334.

1

The Propositional Impasse

> Modern theology as a whole, conservative and liberal, is a long series of debates over which set of concepts—which "-isms"—best names and thinks God. . . . Modern theology is overdependent on a single form: *dedramatized propositions*, statements about God taken out of their context in the economy of divine communicative action.
>
> —Kevin Vanhoozer, *The Drama of Doctrine*

In a *New York Times* op-ed article, Sam Polk confessed that he had a wealth addiction problem. Speaking about one year in particular, he said, "My bonus was $3.6 million—and I was angry because it wasn't big enough."[1] No doubt, this anger contributed to his self-realization. Such a public acknowledgment, though, is nothing unusual except for what happened next. Determined to overcome his money addiction while still relatively young, Sam Polk made the shocking move of quitting his multimillion-dollar Wall Street job. To put in perspective what perks he gave up as a successful hedge fund trader, Polk gives us a glimpse of his old lifestyle:

> I felt so important. At 25, I could go to any restaurant in Manhattan—Per Se, Le Bernardin—just by picking up the phone and calling one of my

1. Sam Polk, "For the Love of Money," *New York Times*, January 18, 2014, https://www.nytimes.com/2014/01/19/opinion/sunday/for-the-love-of-money.html.

> brokers, who ingratiate themselves to traders by entertaining with unlimited expense accounts. I could be second row at the Knicks-Lakers game just by hinting to a broker I might be interested in going. The satisfaction wasn't just about the money. It was about the power.[2]

While decisive and admirable, Polk's dramatic act did not come without the price of an addiction withdrawal. He wrote,

> Despite my realizations, it was incredibly difficult to leave. I was terrified of running out of money and of forgoing future bonuses. More than anything, I was afraid that five or 10 years down the road, I'd feel like an idiot for walking away from my one chance to be really important. What made it harder was that people thought I was crazy for thinking about leaving.[3]

Yet, somehow, he did it. He overcame his addiction and his withdrawals. Ultimately, he even started his own nonprofit corporation to serve underprivileged families. An inspiring act, indeed!

Many young college students have sought Polk's guidance for their own career so that they might avoid the pitfall of becoming addicted to wealth and money. So they ask him: If they follow Polk's noble example, would they still be able to provide for their family? In short, who would take care of them and their loved ones if they did the right thing? Polk's response is quite revealing and illuminating of his own perception of what extricated him from wealth addiction. Responding to the question from his own personal experience, Polk encouraged these up-and-coming leaders of our society to "have faith that something would come, that the universe would provide" for them and their family as they pursue the right priorities in life.[4] To Polk, the universe came through for him and will also come through for these young people.

From a Christian standpoint, Sam Polk is correct to say that somehow human needs will be provided for. But the Christian worldview differs from his understanding of the source from which our help comes. It is

2. Polk, quoted in Lauren Lyster, "This Wall Street Trader Was Making Millions by 30 and Left It All Behind, Here's Why," Yahoo, https://finance.yahoo.com/blogs/daily-ticker/this-guy-had-made-more-than--5-million-on-wall-street-by-30-and-left-it-all--here-s-why-175020255.html.

3. Polk, "For the Love of Money."

4. Quoted in Lyster, "This Wall Street Trader Was Making Millions."

not an impersonal universe but a personal God who provides. It is in this very scenario that the Christian doctrine of providence distinguishes itself from other ways of understanding providence. Not fate or chance or luck or anything else has been providing for all of our needs. Rather, it is the triune God of the Bible.

Indeed, Sam Polk's mistaken attribution to an impersonal universe as the source of human provision is nothing new. Michael Horton says that during the Enlightenment, the "Christian doctrine of providence became secularized as a myth of an immanent and inevitable historical progress" that has stayed with us today.[5] Or as Michael Sandel succinctly puts it, today we have "a providentialism without God."[6] Yet, the proper posture is spelled out in what Moses once commanded the children of Israel: "When you have eaten and are satisfied, you shall bless the Lord your God for the good land which He has given you" (Deut. 8:10). Why? Verse 17 anticipates this question with the answer: "You may say in your heart, 'My power and the strength of my hand made me this wealth.'" But Moses goes on to remind them, "It is He who is giving you power to make wealth" (v. 18). There is, then, no such thing as a Godless providentialism in the Christian worldview.

The Sam Polk incident shows us that the modern world is impressed with and wants to replicate his character for the betterment of our society. But an important ingredient eludes us. Where can we find the inner wherewithal and confidence to bring about such bold and adventurous individuals? It is precisely on this point that the Christian doctrine of providence must be articulated again and again to every generation so that more Sam Polks can be produced with the proper biblical motivation to accompany the lifestyle.

General Agreement on the Doctrine of Providence

It is not unusual for readers of the Bible to derive various interpretations on any number of issues. This phenomenon is no different when it comes

5. Horton, *Christian Faith*, 355.

6. Sandel, *Tyranny of Merit*, 42. Earlier, G. K. Chesterton similarly observed, with a tinge of sarcasm, America's distorted notion of its progress: "Progress is Providence without God. That is, it is a theory that everything has always perpetually gone right by accident. It is a sort of atheistic optimism, based on an everlasting coincidence far more miraculous than a miracle." *What I Saw in America*, 246.

to the doctrine of providence. Diversity of viewpoints is not to be despised but rather cherished as an indication of the richness of insights that divine revelation yields. That human minds cannot agree upon or harmonize everything revealed in Scripture does not diminish the grandeur of God but rather testifies to it.

Interestingly, when it comes to the doctrine of providence, there is actually a core working agreement among Bible scholars on what Scripture has to say about the subject. The following is a brief summary of their doctrinal agreement on divine providence.

What Is Providence?

The word "providence" comes from the Latin word *providere*, meaning "to see beforehand."[7] When used in theology, the term means more than just God passively watching events in history unfold. Rather, it connotes the idea that because God "sees" the plight of humanity ahead of time, he makes his decisions to act on their behalf accordingly. Providence in the Bible comes to mean the actions that God takes in the care of his creation.

While the term "providence" itself is not found in the Bible, the concept is clearly replete in Scripture. The incident that comes closest to the Bible's direct usage of the term "providence" is found in Genesis 22. When God commanded Abraham to sacrifice his only son, Isaac, as a test of his faith, Abraham obeyed without hesitation. On their way to Mount Moriah, Isaac was unaware that he was supposed to be the sacrifice and asked Abraham, "Behold, the fire and the wood, but where is the lamb for the burnt offering?" (v. 7). Abraham responded, "God will provide for Himself the lamb for the burnt offering, my son" (v. 8). When the time came for Abraham to sacrifice Isaac, God put a stop to the test and, indeed, provided a ram caught in a thicket to take the place of Isaac as the sacrifice. Because of God's provision, "Abraham called the name of that place The Lord Will Provide" (v. 14). This incident demonstrates the kind of God Yahweh is: he is "Jehovah Jireh" (the God who provides). Genesis 22 then serves as a locus classicus for the doctrine of providence. It not only gives biblical warrant for the usage of the term "providence" but also endorses the very pursuit of the theological inquiry before us now.

7. Rule, "Providence and Preservation," 76.

Ultimately, though, providence is not just a manifestation of God's raw power of intervention. To properly grasp the biblical concept of providence, one must see in the doctrine, at least, the following troika of divine attributes at work: (1) God as all-loving, (2) God as all-wise, and (3) God as all-powerful. The harmonious outworking of these three, among other attributes, is what produces a balanced articulation of the biblical doctrine of providence.

The Theological Elements of Providence

While the three key divine attributes serve as the conceptual bedrock of divine action, theologians through the years have also interwoven them into a formulaic way of articulating the doctrine of providence. There are basically two formal elements that comprise the doctrine of providence. Generally speaking, Christian theologians across different theological traditions agree on these two: preservation and governance.

First, by preservation we mean that God keeps all things he created existing. He maintains their properties so that they go on functioning as he intended them to. Note that Hebrews 1:3 states that Jesus Christ "upholds all things by the word of His power." The implication is that if he should ever let go of the universe, everything would fall apart and disintegrate. Nehemiah 9:6 is even more explicit in using the term "preserve." Nehemiah declares in his prayer, "You are the Lord, you alone. You have made heaven, the heaven of heavens, with all their host, the earth and all that is on it, the seas and all that is in them; and you preserve all of them; and the host of heaven worships you" (ESV).

In asserting that God preserves all things, one has to quickly add that this is no mechanical or mindless maintenance of the status quo. By preserving what he has created, God is demonstrating also his great love and wisdom toward it. In other words, bound up in his preservation activity is not only his omnipotence but also his great benevolence and wise purposes for humankind.

Second, by governance we mean that God, who is the governor of the world, directs all things in order that they accomplish his good purposes. The emphasis here is on his active involvement in the affairs of creation according to his intentions. Nothing can thwart his will as the sovereign governor of the world. Psalm 103:19 makes this clear: "The Lord has established His throne in the heavens, and His sovereignty rules over all." Ephesians 1:11 further elaborates that God "works all things after the counsel of His will."

Through God's providence of governance, Christian theology is also asserting that history is going somewhere. And where it goes is in the direction God intends it to go. Again, when God exercises this kind of providence, he does so as a way of manifesting his power, wisdom, and love for humanity.

Thus far, there is nothing controversial or disagreeable among the different Christian traditions on these two formal elements of providence. Indeed, there is actually agreement across denominations, such that Roger Olson can remark,

> Based on these revelatory themes [stated above and in the Bible] as well as on clear, logical deduction from the very nature of God as both great and good, the early church fathers, medieval thinkers, Protestant Reformers and post-Reformation Christian scholars and theologians all in chorus expressed the consensual Christian belief that nature and history are sovereignly, providentially governed by God and nothing happens or can happen without God's permission.[8]

The Purpose of the Doctrine of Providence

It is important to note that the purpose and the overall "mood" of the doctrine of providence is one of comfort and reassurance. The apostle James writes, "Every good thing given and every perfect gift is from above, coming down from the Father of lights, with whom there is no variation or shifting shadow" (James 1:17). That being true, we must always see everything good that comes our way as part of God's good providence for us. To properly grasp the doctrine of providence, one must embrace the theological presupposition of *Deus pro nobis* ("God for us"). This is the heart of the doctrine of providence.

"Belief in providence," T. J. Gorringe observes, "is not a belief required of us formally by the creeds but, much more profoundly, by our daily prayer."[9] In this way, the doctrine of providence carries with it an animat-

8. Olson, *Mosaic of Christian Belief*, 181.
9. Gorringe, *God's Theatre*, 1.

ing force that causes us to live an active life of meaning and significance in the world. For, as Gorringe insightfully explains,

> Belief in providence is the very structure of the religious life: belief that God acts, that he has a purpose not simply for the whole of creation but for me, that this purpose can be discerned and that, through prayer, I can put myself in the way of it. It is also the belief that I can bring every concern to God, from the wars and famines I read about in the newspaper or see on the news to the relationship difficulties I encounter, or the problems with my work, in the conviction that this will make a difference.[10]

In agreement with Gorringe, the famous radio Bible teacher J. Vernon McGee puts it even more bluntly and prosaically:

> I would quit preaching if it were not for the providence of God. His providence is what makes life thrilling and exciting. Neither you nor I know what is around the corner, but God by His providence is leading. . . . Every day is a new adventure for the child of God. He brings into our lives enemies and trouble, but He also brings sweetness and love, blessings, light, and abundant life.[11]

It is this belief in providence, therefore, that animates the Christian's life and turns the vicissitudes of life into an adventure together with God.

Sadly, though, belief in providence is not currently held in high regard within evangelicalism, much less outside of it. For the consensus on the doctrine has been meager, and the disagreements have widened within Christian traditions. And this theological trend in the doctrine, unless halted and addressed, will threaten to undermine what Gorringe describes as "the very structure of the religious life" of many in the Christian community. The following section explores the reasons for the present condition of the doctrine.

Disagreement, Complexity, and Abstraction in the Doctrine of Providence

Of the two elements in the doctrine of providence, Christians do not seem to disagree about the first element, preservation. The main area of

10. Gorringe, *God's Theatre*, 1.
11. McGee, *Esther*, 20.

disagreement seems to lie with the second element of providence, governance (the sovereignty of God). While no one questions that God governs the world, the bone of contention centers on the extent of that providential governance.

The belief in God's providential governance forms a range or a spectrum of belief. It goes from a weak view[12] to a strong view of God's governance or sovereignty in creation. The two basic schools of thought that form the two poles within the theological range or spectrum of providence are Calvinism and Arminianism. The former embraces a stronger form of divine governance in providence, while the latter employs a weaker or milder form.

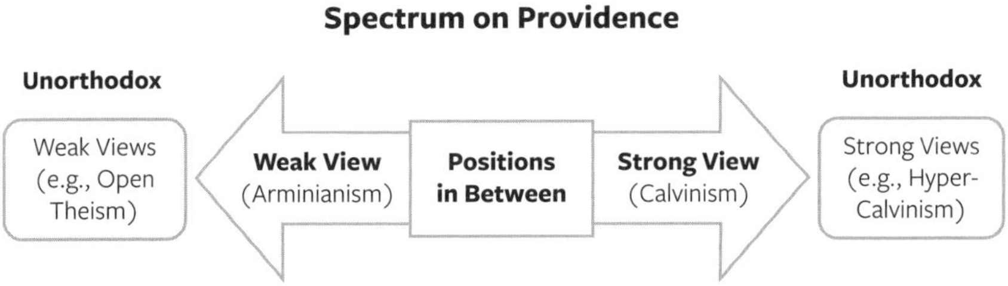

Spectrum on Providence

Unorthodox
Weak Views (e.g., Open Theism)

Weak View (Arminianism)

Positions in Between

Strong View (Calvinism)

Unorthodox
Strong Views (e.g., Hyper-Calvinism)

Figure 1.1

Calvinism is named after John Calvin, the Protestant Reformer from Geneva. But it is somewhat of a misnomer because this view did not originate with him. If we trace it in church history, it is more precise perhaps to ascribe this view to the fourth-century church father Augustine. Be that as it may, it was Calvin and those who followed his Reformed teachings who popularized and propagated this strong view of God's governance or sovereignty. So, this is where the theological emphasis got its moniker.

Arminianism is named after Jacob Arminius, a former Calvinist, who opposed the strong way of understanding God's governance in the world.[13] Like Calvinism, there are those who would say that Arminius's view did

12. This is not necessarily a pejorative. Rather, it is simply following the taxonomy given by Roger Olson, who is an adherent of this position. See Olson, *Against Calvinism*, 71.

13. The main contention of Arminianism against Calvinism is often focused in the area of soteriology (the doctrine of salvation). Naturally, though, its overall theological outlook cannot help but also have implications in the broader field of providence.

not originate with him. This view can find support from earlier thinkers in church history.[14] But like Calvinism, it was Arminius and his followers who spread this viewpoint and entered into a formal theological debate with Calvinism on divine sovereignty. Thus, for our purposes, we designate this view as Arminianism.

By no means are these the only two schools of thought when it comes to the doctrine of providence. But these two are major representatives within the spectrum of theological possibilities. Their debate enables the reader to understand other related viewpoints, should the reader choose to explore them further. Needless to say, these two traditions have contributed to the complexity of articulating the doctrine of providence.

To understand the disagreements, complexities, and abstractions that resulted from these schools of thought, we must now examine their views regarding God's governance in two important existential areas of life: (1) divine sovereignty and human free will, and (2) the problem of evil in the world, taken up in the next chapter. Admittedly, these two topics are deserving of their own sustained and in-depth discussion beyond the pages of this book. My intention is not to provide a comprehensive discussion of these two important issues but to simply introduce them to the reader.

The Issue of Divine Sovereignty and Human Free Will

To say that God "governs" his creation implies that he is operating out of a wise and benevolent will that drives his actions in the world. While human beings go about the business of living their lives, wittingly or unwittingly, they interact and contend with this great divine will that is at work all around.

That there is a divine will that governs the world is a given in Christian theological circles. It is undisputed. But there are questions: What kind of divine will? What is the extent of God's governance in this world? What is its relationship to human free will?

14. There were others who preceded Arminius in the articulation of his theological position. Roger Olson asserts that Jacob Arminius's teaching did not originate with him. Others such as Balthasar Hubmaier articulated the same beliefs before Arminius. Olson, *Arminianism FAQ*, 1. A. A. Hodge thinks that Pelagius, or a modified teaching of Pelagius known as semi-Pelagianism which came before Arminius, finds kinship with Arminius's teachings. Hodge, *Outlines in Theology*, 334–35.

The Calvinist View of God's Governance

Looking at the theological spectrum of God's providential governance, we see that the dominant or older school of thought known as Calvinism represents a strong view of God's providence of governance. John Calvin, whose name this viewpoint bears, makes plain "that all events are governed by God's secret plan."[15] Unwilling to let chance or fate or the stars or anything outside of God have the controlling word on the affairs of creation, Calvin goes on to say, "Let him, therefore, who would beware of this infidelity ever remember that there is no erratic power, or action, or motion in creatures, but that they are governed by God's secret plan in such a way that nothing happens except what is knowingly and willingly decreed by him."[16] Similarly, Thomas Aquinas says, "When the free will moves itself, this does not exclude its being moved by another [i.e., God], from whom it receives the very power to move itself."[17] To underscore Calvin and Aquinas's point, R. C. Sproul makes this pithy statement: "There are no maverick molecules in a universe where God is sovereign."[18] Everything that moves in this world does so under the governance of a sovereign God.

It would be easy to assume that such a strong viewpoint of God's governance has no room for human free will. But it does. The following are three ways Calvinism demonstrates the importance of human free will within its system of thought despite a strong, meticulous notion of divine governance.

First, Calvinism simply affirms the clear biblical teaching of the Bible that human beings are called to make moral choices. The biblical record is replete with instances of humans being commanded to make the right choice, especially to choose between God and his ways and our own sinful ways. This, then, presupposes human free will. Without human free will, there can be no theodrama that constitutes the human and divine relationship in the world whereby humans respond to God's injunctions. A. A. Hodge says, "This matter of free will underlies everything. . . .

15. Calvin, *Institutes* 1.16.2 (1:199).

16. Calvin, *Institutes* 1.16.3 (1:201).

17. Thomas Aquinas, *Summa theologiae* I.83.1 (1:418), quoted in Horton, *Christian Faith*, 357.

18. R. C. Sproul, "Chosen by God," Ligonier Ministries, https://www.ligonier.org/learn/series/chosen-by-god/gods-sovereignty.

Everything is gone if free-will is gone; the moral system is gone if free-will is gone."[19]

Indeed, it is precisely because humans have this ability to make their moral choices that God is said to be just and righteous when he judges us for obedience or disobedience to his commandments. Moreover, not only must humans be free to make their moral choices, but also God cannot be controlling the evil or wicked actions of humans. In other words, the Calvinist position understands that God cannot be directly acting to promote the very evil he commands us to avoid. Otherwise, this would compromise his standing as a holy and righteous judge.

Second, the Calvinist position employs the concept of concurrence to help clarify its view of how divine sovereignty and human free will work together. In concurrence, providence is understood as God cooperating "with created things in the very action, directing their distinctive properties to cause them to act as they do."[20]

From a positive point of view—that is, when good things happen in life—concurrence is seen as God's way of providing for humanity through his divine instruments or agents. God does not personally deliver our daily bread right up to our doorstep. Rather, it is done through indirect means, usually through the instrumentality of other human beings or created order, or even the very sweat from our own brows that he enabled us to exert. In receiving these goods in this manner, we acknowledge that it was God working concurrently with the actions of other created things that meet our needs. Martin Luther refers to the action of these individuals as the "masks" of God in caring for our needs.[21]

Note in Psalm 104:14–15 how seamlessly the psalmist depicts the actions of God and the actions of human beings working together to provide for human needs:

> He causes the grass to grow for the cattle,
> And vegetation for the labor of man,
> So that he may bring forth food from the earth,
> And wine which makes man's heart glad,

19. A. A. Hodge, *Evangelical Theology* (1890), quoted in Carson, *Divine Sovereignty*, 207.
20. Grudem, *Systematic Theology*, 317.
21. Luther, "Exposition of Psalm 147."

> So that he may make his face glisten with oil,
> And food which sustains man's heart.

This mutual cooperation, while involving creaturely actions, is seen as God's gracious act for which we are to praise him. This is what is meant by concurrence.

Concurrence, then, is a logical extension of divine preservation and governance manifested practically and daily in our creaturely existence. It highlights in a very specific way God's role in bringing about the good that comes our way, thereby eliciting our praise to him and causing us to cast all of our cares on him (1 Pet. 5:7).

Now, Calvinists, of course, know that concurrence can also be viewed from a negative point of view—that is, when bad things happen in life. In such a situation, they appeal to James 1:13, where the apostle James explicitly instructs, "Let no one say when he is tempted, 'I am being tempted by God'; for God cannot be tempted by evil, and He Himself does not tempt anyone." So, based on that biblical teaching, most Calvinists would deny that God is connected to evil even as they uphold God's concurrence in all events that happen in the world. In short, God's concurring sovereignty is not seen as symmetrical when dealing with good events versus evil events in the world. How Calvinists explain this is dealt with in depth in my discussion of the problem of evil in chapter 2.

Third, the Calvinist position shows that it makes room for human free will by recognizing that the Bible mentions instances of God granting humans permission to act as they wish even if it runs contrary to his will. Here, God deliberately makes way for humans to decide and act in a given situation—especially in cases dealing with evil—without unduly influencing human choices. Thus, through the means of divine "permission," what humans decide to do is done freely and yet not outside the control of God's providential governance, since he gave them permission to decide as they wish.

Major Criticism of the Calvinist View and Its Response

What is stated above demonstrates the Calvinist commitment to uphold the notion of human free will. But there are objections to the Calvinist way of articulating human free will. To be sure, opposition comes from the Arminian school of thought. Interestingly, though, the criticism at times also comes even from within the Calvinist camp.

One such glaring example is when it comes to the idea of divine "permission." At first glance, one would assume that we know what Calvinists mean by that term. But upon closer examination, the Calvinist understanding of divine permission is not as simple as it looks. It is safe to say that it is not the conventional way most people understand the term. Calvinists, however, would argue that because we are dealing with a transcendent being like God, "permission" must be adjusted to fit the divine subject at hand.[22]

In the Calvinist way of construing divine permission, it is true that God has given humans "permission" to decide and to act as they see fit. However, since God has the attribute of omniscience (all-knowingness), he has to know in advance what those human choices and actions eventually will become. Moreover, he also knows how he himself would react or respond to those human decisions ahead of time. And, based on this knowledge that he possesses, he inevitably "makes certain" or "insures" or "guarantees" that those things will happen exactly as he knows them to happen in due time. But, if this is true, this would also mean that human beings, while given permission to act in the way they wish, in actuality cannot change their mind or do anything different from what God already knew would happen. In effect, this divine foreknowledge—which involves God's decision ahead of time to either intervene or not—is his sovereign decree or secret will on a given situation. And, in a sense, it serves as the final word. Humans cannot do anything to produce a different outcome.

"Permission," then, enables the human decision-makers to act as they wish, but, from God's standpoint, the human choice has already been taken into account within his sovereign decree. Thus, John Feinberg summarizes well the Calvinist position: "God includes whatever means are necessary to accomplish his ends in a way that avoids constraining the agent to do what is decreed. Human actions are thus causally determined but free."[23] Feinberg, though, is quick to assert that Calvinism is not the

22. "The idea of permission is always qualified as being active in nature, and as forming no limitation to God's purposeful activity. Divine permission is, in fact, meant by Reformed theology as a work of Divine majesty." Berkouwer, *Providence of God*, 150.

23. Feinberg, "God Ordains All Things," 29. He also says, "I hold that God is absolutely sovereign, and thus possesses absolute self-determination. This means that God's will covers all

same as fatalism or hard determinism, whereby humans are forced to do what they did not want to do. That's because God has given humankind "permission," as Calvinists delineated the meaning of that term when it comes to God. No doubt, this peculiar Calvinist usage of the term "permission" carries with it a measure of theological complexity that one must embrace to fully understand.

Sometimes, though, the way this Calvinist concept of permission is articulated comes very close to denying the existence of human free will in order to uphold a strong view of God's sovereignty. For instance, when discussing permission, John Calvin says, "Men can accomplish nothing except by God's secret command. . . . They cannot by deliberating accomplish anything except what he has already decreed with himself and determines by his secret direction."[24] To demonstrate how this process works, Calvin elaborates:

> As far as pertains to those secret promptings we are discussing, Solomon's statement that the heart of a king is turned about hither and thither at God's pleasure [Prov. 21:1] certainly extends to all the human race, and carries as much weight as if he had said: "Whatever we conceive of in our minds is directed to his own end by God's secret inspiration."[25]

In this portrayal of such a close nexus between God and human decision-making, one cannot help but admire its strong commitment to divine sovereignty. But one is also compelled to wonder if there is even such a thing as human free will anymore—even within the auspices of divine permission. Despite Feinberg's denial of fatalism, Calvinism sure comes very close to it at times in its articulation of providence.

Not all Calvinists, therefore, are convinced that the depiction of a human will overpowered or infused by the divine will in every instance of human decision-making is a satisfactory way of understanding divine permission. Charles Hodge is one such leading Calvinist theologian who criticized this approach, especially when God is seen as the concurring force working directly

---

things and that the basis for God's sovereign choice is not what God foresees will happen nor anything else external to his will. Rather, God's good pleasure and good purposes determine what he decrees. I also believe that God has chosen at once the whole interconnected sequence of events and actions that have and will occur in our world" (29).

24. Calvin, *Institutes* 1.18.1 (1:229).

25. Calvin, *Institutes* 1.18.2 (1:231).

to produce every human decision or action. Hodge says that he does not deny that God is sovereignly at work providentially in human affairs. However, how God works in conjunction with human free will is "unrevealed and inscrutable" in the Bible. It is, therefore, best to "rest satisfied with the simple statement that preservation is that omnipotent energy of God" that enables his creatures to do what they do—good or bad—without getting into the specific explanation of how concurrence or permission works.[26] Likewise, G. C. Berkouwer observes that human nature seems to "want to know 'how this [the intricacies of providence] is done.' But such knowledge is out of the question, since 'the mode of God's action we cannot possibly understand.'"[27]

For Arminians, the unconventional way Calvinists understand divine "permission" and their concept of concurrence simply shows that there is no real free will within the Calvinist school of thought. Rightly or wrongly, Arminians see Calvinism as portraying humans as nothing more than puppets on a string controlled by a divine puppeteer. It certainly does not help when Calvinists themselves, in an effort to ascribe to God complete sovereignty, do not bother, at times, to nuance between human action and God's action in a given event.

Roger Olson cites the incident of a leading Calvinist who came to Olson's university chapel and shared about the tragic death of his son in a mountain climbing accident. The Calvinist speaker said several times in his talk, "God killed my son." "The speaker made crystal clear what he meant. He did *not* mean God permitted his son's death or merely allowed it to happen. Rather, he meant that God planned it and rendered it certain."[28] As Olson recalls, the Calvinist speaker further explained that "every such death, like every event, is planned and governed by God in such a way as to make it inevitable."[29] To that end, instead of seeing God as a majestic monarch, as most Calvinists do, Arminians like Olson actually see this portrait of God as a cruel tyrant, something to be rejected for its depiction of God that is incompatible with that of Scripture.

26. Hodge, *Systematic Theology*, 1:581.

27. Berkouwer, *Providence of God*, 140, quoting Hodge, *Systematic Theology*, 2:604ff.

28. Olson, *Against Calvinism*, 70.

29. Olson, *Against Calvinism*, 70. To be fair, Olson also mentions the Calvinist speaker's rationale. "It was the only thing that brought him comfort and hope in the face of such a shattering tragedy. If his son's death was merely an accident and not part of God's plan, he said, he could not live with the utter randomness and meaninglessness of it. He could only find comfort in his son's death *if* it was God's doing and not at all an accident" (71).

The Arminian View of God's Governance

Opposite the Calvinist position, the Arminian school of thought takes a weak or mild form of God's providential governance in the world. By doing this, it emphasizes the role of human beings in shaping world events without necessarily denying God's role in it. The classic Arminian position is to view God's providential governance as present but not overly intrusive in world affairs. The main driving explanation for why events happen is that human beings cause them to happen due to their God-given free will. And God, while sovereign and possessing a divine plan, does not interfere with the exercise of human choices lest they no longer be free choices.

If this is all that the Arminian position entails, it really does not distinguish itself that much from the Calvinist position. What the Arminians state above could easily be affirmed by many Calvinists as well. So, Jack Cottrell provides us with a key Arminian distinctive.

In a succinct way, Cottrell describes how God governs the world and yet does so without infringing upon human free will: through his foreknowledge. Through his omniscience of what will happen in the future and, specifically, how humans will decide or act in a given situation, God can then formulate in advance what he will do in response to the human exercise of their free will. Therefore, God's "foreknowledge is grounded in—and is thus conditioned by—the [human] choices themselves as foreknown" by God.[30] In the subtle use of God's foreknowledge, Cottrell depicts the typical Arminian understanding of "how God maintains sovereign control over the whole of his creation, despite the freedom he has given his creatures."[31] In short, God plans and acts around what he knows humans will do, thereby maintaining human free will while at the same time asserting his governance of world affairs.

The advantage of the Arminian school of thought is that this position has the quality of being intuitive. Our instincts naturally agree with this theological framework that we are free creatures who can make our own choices, especially moral ones. It is not that God is too weak to govern the world more forcefully but rather that he chose to withhold or limit his interventions so that human beings can have a measure of autonomy to act freely. Moreover, by downplaying the strong view that God is a divine

30. Cottrell, "Nature of Divine Sovereignty," 111.
31. Cottrell, "Nature of Divine Sovereignty," 111.

monarch who is meticulously in control of everything, the Arminian view of God comes across to us as presenting a more loving, friendly, and accessible deity than the one portrayed by Calvinists.

On the surface, this approach seems to have struck the balance between divine sovereignty and human free will. But it is not without its weak spots and is, therefore, susceptible to criticisms.

Major Criticism of the Arminian View and Its Response

A major criticism of the Arminian position is the seeming powerlessness of the God portrayed in this school of thought when it comes to providence. A lot more emphasis seems to be placed on human decision and action than on God's decision and action. The position tends to be more human-centered than God-centered. The following are some specific points raised against Arminianism.

First, Calvinists would press the Arminians for a clarification on the nature of human free will that they are referring to. In other words, human free will and its usage is conditioned on whether we are referring to a pre-fall world or a post-fall world—that is, a world unstained by sin or a world dominated by sin. Since humans can act only according to their nature, this factor is key to our understanding of human free will. In the state of innocence found in a pre-fallen world—as Adam and Eve were in the garden of Eden—humanity could be expected to decide whether to choose to do good or evil. But in a post-fallen world, where human nature is now infected with sin, despite a God-given choice, it can be expected that the human will can choose to do only that which is consistent with its sinful nature. Thus, humankind will almost always "freely" choose to go against God's commands unless he plays a more active role in his providential governance that includes his gracious intervention in the exercise of human will.

Humanity, therefore, is like an addict who is, technically speaking, free to say no to his addiction but is in reality unable to do so. Borrowing from the addiction imagery, we might say that God has to then stage his creative interventions on behalf of humanity in his governance. For this reason, Calvinists insist that God cannot be passive but must be active in his providential governance if humankind is to do anything truly good and worthwhile. And to that extent, whenever humankind chooses the right decision and action, all praise and glory deservedly go to God for his role in it.

In view of this criticism, the usual Arminian response is to acknowledge that humans are indeed fallen in sin. However, God has given humanity "prevenient grace," whereby humans are able to make the right choices despite their fallen human condition. This prevenient grace is made available at the first advent of Jesus Christ, who is the "true Light which, coming into the world, enlightens every man" (John 1:9). Indeed, some Arminians go so far as to view prevenient grace as effectively eradicating the fallen state of humankind so that what is left for them to do is to make the right choices in life because of the reality of prevenient grace.[32]

If prevenient grace can, indeed, be established as a solid biblical teaching, then it would go a long way toward supporting the Arminian idea that God does not have to be as active in his governance as Calvinists think he should. But this is surely disputed not only by Calvinists but even by some Arminians. Arminian theologian Clark Pinnock questioned the biblical basis for the kind of prevenient grace espoused by traditional Arminians. He says, "The Bible has no developed doctrine of universal prevenient grace, however convenient it would be for us [Arminians] if it did."[33] That is why in upholding a weak form of divine governance, Pinnock chooses instead to deny the doctrine of total depravity (all humankind is infected with sin) rather than to argue for the biblical basis of prevenient grace. Whether by bringing in the idea of prevenient grace or denying human depravity, Arminianism has had to contend with the sinfulness of humankind in its assertion that people are truly free to make the right choices given them by God.

Second, Arminians themselves see in the classical Arminian position an inconsistency that renders it just as deterministic as Calvinism. "On the Arminian portrait of God," Richard Rice says, "providence is not the inexorable outworking of an invariant plan established in eternity. It is God's creative response to events as they happen, based on his perfect anticipation of the future and his infinite capacity to work for good in every situation."[34] But, as it stands right now, the Arminian articulation of

32. Lewis and Demarest, *Integrative Theology*, 187.
33. Pinnock, "From Augustine to Arminius," 22.
34. Rice, "Divine Foreknowledge," 136.

providence contains a key element that has a determinative effect. What is that theological element that is deterministic? It is, surprisingly, the cornerstone of Arminian understanding of divine sovereignty: God's attribute of foreknowledge. Richard Rice explains:

> The concept of absolute foreknowledge retained from Calvinism is incompatible with the dynamic portrait of God that is basic to Arminianism. Absolute foreknowledge—the idea that God sees the entire future in advance—is incompatible with the concept that God interacts with his creatures on a momentary basis. If God knows everything that will ever happen, including all our future decisions, then the actual occurrence of events contributes nothing to his experience. He already enjoys whatever value they have, along with that of his reaction to them.[35]

In viewing this argument for a consistent indeterminacy, some Arminians felt compelled to reject the attribute of divine foreknowledge as it is traditionally understood within Christian orthodoxy in order to make room for human free will.

Those who follow the lead of people such as Clark Pinnock, Richard Rice, John Sanders, Greg Boyd, and Thomas Oord call themselves Open Theists and embrace the view that the future is open to God; that is, God does not know the future especially in regard to how human beings will use their free choice. But, as one can quickly see, this view runs counter not only to the traditional understanding of God but also to the biblical view of God. God's omniscience and, therefore, his perfect foreknowledge have always been part of the Christian teaching of who God is. These orthodox attributes of God seem to be the price one has to pay to become a consistent Arminian. But for many Arminians, it is too high a price, and they are willing to face the scorn of their fellow Arminians for their being "inconsistent" Arminians.[36]

35. Rice, "Divine Foreknowledge," 133.

36. As an alternative to Open Theism, some Arminian theologians have gravitated to middle knowledge, sometimes known as Molinism (named after sixteenth-century Jesuit theologian Luis de Molina). This view states that because God is all-wise, he therefore knows all counterfactuals. Like a master chess player, he could anticipate with a great deal of precision how a person would exercise free will or choice in a given situation. In this way, God still rules without overreaching into human free will. But, like Open Theism, this view falls short of saying that God possesses the kind of foreknowledge that traditional Arminians and, indeed, orthodox Christians through the centuries have always understood him to have.

Third, there is in Arminianism a hesitancy concerning the portrayal of God as monarch, if not an outright rejection of the concept. Thus, Arminians see that God's modus operandi (normal mode of operation) is to let humans decide the course of action without interfering in any sense of the word. Indeed, in many instances, God's eternal or decretive will is held to a minimum or, in certain cases,[37] is even nonexistent. There seems to be a deliberate effort to not think about God's role in determining certain outcomes. This is especially true with dark and unpleasant events in history. As Clark Pinnock confesses, "In the past, I would slip into my reading of the Bible dark assumptions about the nature of God's decrees and intentions. What a relief to be done with them!"[38]

While commendable in its portrayal of a generous and nonautocratic notion of God, such a theological posture opens itself up to criticism regarding the notion that God is not fully in control of events in the world. Because God is not really the monarch of the universe in the Arminian theological outlook, one cannot help but wonder if human decisions and actions are, ultimately, the final arbiter of events in the created order. Arminianism's position is de facto similar to William Ernest Henley's poem "Invictus,"[39] in which the poet states,

> Out of the night that covers me,
> Black as the Pit from pole to pole,
> I thank whatever gods may be
> For my unconquerable soul.
>
> In the fell clutch of circumstance
> I have not winced nor cried aloud.
> Under the bludgeonings of chance
> My head is bloody, but unbowed.
>
> Beyond this place of wrath and tears
> Looms but the Horror of the shade,

37. By "certain cases" I am thinking of bad or evil events that have happened. Often, instead of wrestling with how they relate back to God, they are simply understood as the result of human or creaturely free-will actions but not necessarily coming from a divine source or having any divine connection at all.

38. Pinnock, "From Augustine to Arminius," 21.

39. William Ernest Henley, "Invictus," available at https://www.poetryfoundation.org/poems/51642/invictus.

And yet the menace of the years
Finds, and shall find, me unafraid.

It matters not how strait the gate,
How charged with punishments the scroll,
I am the master of my fate:
I am the captain of my soul.

When God always defers to human decisions and actions, it is not God who runs the affairs of the world but rather humans, who make themselves the captains of their own souls.

The following real-life incident illustrates the problem inherent within the Arminian concept of a God deferential toward human action instead of his own counsel. The setting is the time of the Mexican-American War. Captain John Coffee "Jack" Hays and the Texas Rangers were surrounded by enemy forces. As the story goes, before they went to battle, Captain Hays led the troops in prayer, whereby he said,

> O Lord, we are about to join battle with a vastly superior number of the enemy, and, Heavenly Father, we would mighty like for you to be on our side and help us. But if You can't do it, for Christ's sake don't go over to the Mexicans, just lie low and keep in the dark, and You will see one of the dangest fights You've ever seen.[40]

And instead of saying "Amen" to finish the prayer (which means, of course, "Let it be" or "So be it according to God's will"), he simply roared, "Charge!"[41] And so they went to battle.

We are amused and shocked at the same time by the seeming irreverence of Captain Jack Hays's prayer. But, most of all, we cannot help but realize how biblically naive the prayer is, since there would be no way for God to just stand on the sideline. Is there really ever a situation where God has no knowledge or input in a historical outcome?

In its place, one might be reminded of another incident, this time involving Abraham Lincoln during the Civil War. It was alleged that one of his advisers said openly that he was grateful that God was on their side. Not wanting to be presumptuous, the president gave another perspective

40. Phares, *Bible in Pocket*, 136.
41. Phares, *Bible in Pocket*, 136.

as a corrective. "Sir, my concern is not whether God is on our side," Lincoln said. "My greatest concern is to be on God's side, for God is always right."[42] Such is also the force of the Calvinist critique of the Arminian position. Providence centers not on the human side of the equation but on the divine side.

42. Joe Carter, "Being on God's Side: An Open Letter to the Religious Right," *First Things*, December 22, 2010, https://www.firstthings.com/web-exclusives/2010/12/being-on-gods-side-an-open-letter-to-the-religious-right.

2

The Problem of Evil Impasse

> Is God willing to prevent evil, but not able? Then he is not omnipotent.
> Is he able, but not willing? Then he is malevolent.
> Is he both able and willing? Then whence cometh evil?
> Is he neither able nor willing? Then why call him God?
>
> —Epicurus

The Problem of Evil

Another important area where God's providence of governance is passionately discussed between Calvinists and Arminians is the problem of evil. Since God is providentially governing his creation, how can this created order be filled with so much pain and suffering? Why is there evil in the world?

Theologian Robert Culver observes that, generally, people are not offended when we attribute to God the inclement weather that kept Napoleon's troops from conquering Europe or the calmness of the English Channel that allowed the British army to escape destruction from Hitler's pursuit at Dunkirk. We actually thank him for his *active* role in our world. "But," he says, "few approve the suggestion that the Chicago fire may have been caused by God, especially when the cow of a careless Irish housewife can be blamed. What about the San Francisco earthquake, or the floods and quakes in China?"[1]

What Culver raises is popularly known as the problem of evil. In many ways, this issue is built upon my prior discussion of divine sovereignty and human free will. The problem of evil is a more involved discussion of divine sovereignty and human free will centering on the specific issue of evil.

Addressing the problem of evil is important because this issue has a tendency to either confirm or invalidate the doctrine of providence in the minds of people. But, as we will see in this section, it will take more than just intellectually addressing the problem of evil to truly captivate minds and hearts toward the Bible's teaching on providence.

Biblical Starting Point

A natural human tendency is to attribute evil and its manifestations to an omnipotent God. After all, what greater power or force could there be in the created order than him? Everything emanates from him. While this sentiment is understandable, the apostle James issues a corrective teaching that forms the biblical bedrock for any theological discussion on the problem of evil:

> Let no one say when he is tempted, "I am being tempted by God"; for God cannot be tempted by evil, and He Himself does not tempt anyone. But each one is tempted when he is carried away and enticed by his own lust. Then when lust has conceived, it gives birth to sin; and when sin is accomplished, it brings forth death. Do not be deceived, my beloved brethren. (James 1:13–16)

No matter how sovereign or all-powerful we conceive God to be, one of the things we must not think of him is that he is so omnipotent that he is also the author of evil who tempts us to sin (v. 13). It cannot be. For this would be contrary to his attribute of holiness. Instead, we must see the root of all evil in the world as arising from the human heart carried away by its own lusts toward sinful deeds (vv. 14–15). Thus, James warns

1. Culver, *The Living God*, 137.

that if we think of God as being different from what James instructs, we "deceive" ourselves into a false concept of him (v. 16). That's because, in providence, it is not only God's power to govern creation that is put on display, but also his goodness and wisdom. We must, therefore, be careful to demonstrate these divine attributes as working in a balanced harmony.

One would think that such a thorough biblical teaching from the apostle James would settle the issue of the problem of evil once and for all. But not so. The reason goes back to the range or spectrum of God's providential governance discussed earlier.

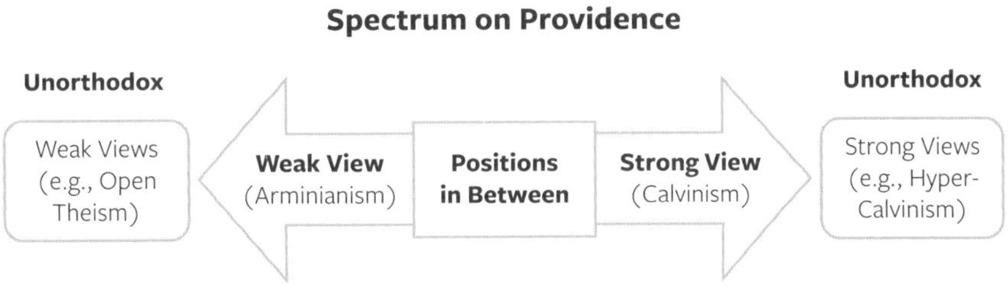

Spectrum on Providence

Unorthodox
Weak Views (e.g., Open Theism)
Weak View (Arminianism)
Positions in Between
Strong View (Calvinism)
Unorthodox
Strong Views (e.g., Hyper-Calvinism)

Figure 2.1

The following discussion gives a sketch of how the different schools of thought understand God's governance as it relates to evil.

The Calvinist School of Thought on the Problem of Evil

Within the spectrum of God's providence, the Calvinist school of thought takes a strong view on God's providential governance. He is sovereign not only in good events but also when things turn bad. For if evil can exist outside of God's governance, then evil is a force or an entity that is capable of an independent existence apart from God. Such a view, however, would not only undermine God's sovereignty in creation but also lead to a view known as ontological dualism—that is, reality as consisting of two kinds of existence: an existence dependent on God and an existence independent of God to which evil belongs. But clearly ontological dualism runs counter to the monotheistic concept of God as depicted in the Bible. There are not two or more independent self-existing entities in the world—that is, there is not more than one God. Everything came into existence because of God, who alone is self-existing and self-sustaining. Thus, for Calvinists, no matter how heinous evil is, its very existence in the world is not outside the control of God's providence and governance.

Despite their commitment to this nondualistic notion of evil, Calvinists are also careful not to fuse evil with the being or the action of God. They are mindful that since the Bible teaches that God is holy, his holiness precludes us from thinking that he has any involvement with evil that comes our way. So, the Calvinist school of thought has the very difficult task of balancing between their strong, nondualistic view of God's sovereignty when it comes to evil and their adherence to the biblical teaching of God's holiness that denies he has any role in evil in the world. How do Calvinists make sense of their position and articulate it in a persuasive way?

One key approach that Calvinists employ to support their view is to make a distinction between ultimate/primary cause and proximate/secondary cause. In every event, there's a chain of causation that has a starting point in time, and it results in a final outcome that constitutes the event at issue.

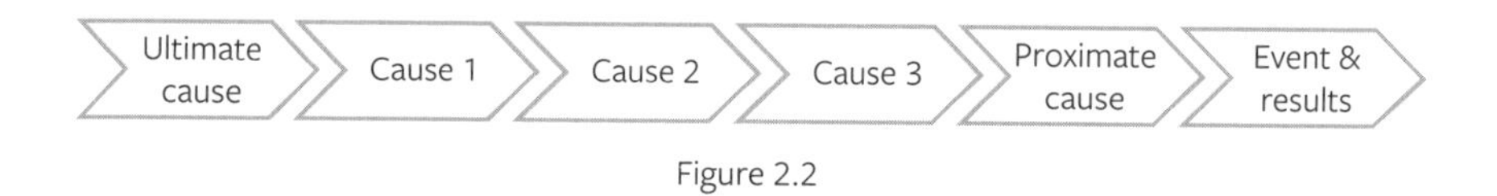

Figure 2.2

The starting point of an event is called the first cause (ultimate cause), which makes possible all actions from that point onward. But subsequent actions carry a distinct role and responsibility in the chain of causation leading to an event. The action closest to an event is known as the proximate cause. It is to the proximate cause alone that we attribute culpability or liability for an unfortunate event and its resulting consequences—even though other causes, such as the first cause, may be part of the chain of causation.

The following is a clarifying illustration. Imagine a man who goes to a car dealership to purchase a brand-new automobile that had just arrived from the manufacturer. Driving the car home from the dealer's lot, the man decides to turn on the fancy sound system in his vehicle. While fiddling with the knobs on the dashboard, he fails to notice that the car ahead has come to a stop. Unable to brake in time, he rear-ends the driver in front of him.

In such a situation, we might ask, "Who or what caused the accident?" Based on our understanding of causation above, the answer to this question would include not just the driver of the car but also the dealer who sold him the car and even the manufacturer that produced the vehicle. For that matter, we could also extend causation all the way back to the teacher who taught the driver how to properly drive a car, or even the parents of the driver who gave birth to him. Without these actors and more, this event could not have happened. They all make up the chain of causation that made possible the event (see fig. 2.3).

It is, however, safe to assume that something else is intended when we ask, "Who or what caused this accident?" In this case, what we really mean to ask is, "Who is culpable or liable for the accident?" Or put another way, we want to know, "Who might the rear-ended driver sue for compensation?" While everyone in the chain of causation is necessary for the event to happen, not everyone is culpable. Determination of culpability rests not merely on being in the chain of causation but on being the "proximate cause." Because the driver of the new car is the proximate cause of the accident, he alone is culpable, not the others in the chain of causation.

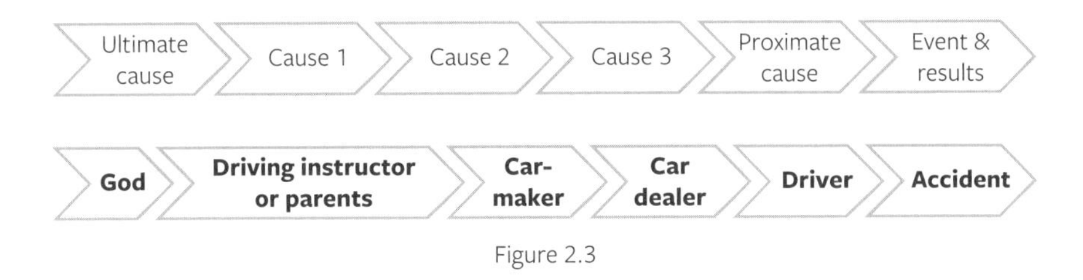

Figure 2.3

God is always the first or the ultimate cause who created everything and, indeed, sustains everything in the created order. This then gives way for humanity and the rest of creation to act as secondary causes. And to the extent that they have acted to bring about evil in the world, they, not God, are potential proximate causes who are culpable for their evil deeds. Looking at it this way, Wayne Grudem summarizes the Calvinist position:

> It is very clear that Scripture nowhere shows God as *directly doing anything evil*, but rather as bringing about evil deeds through the willing actions of moral creatures. . . . However we understand God's relationship to evil, we

> must *never* come to the point where we think that we are not responsible for the evil that we do, or that God takes pleasure in evil or is to be blamed for it. Such a conclusion is clearly contrary to Scripture.[2]

So where did evil come from? Grudem succinctly states, "Evil is actually done not by God but by people or demons who choose to do it."[3] So how then should we describe God's relationship to evil in the world? Grudem explains, "Though God ordained that it would come about, both in general terms and in specific details, yet *God is removed from actually doing evil*, and his bringing it about through 'secondary causes' does not impugn his holiness or render him blameworthy."[4]

In arguing for this position, one can quickly see how Calvinists are balancing between God's providential governance over evil events and his holiness and goodness as seen in the distinction between ultimate and proximate causation. Is their approach persuasive? It certainly is subject to much theological debate today. Not everyone, of course, is satisfied.

The Hyper-Calvinist Minority View

There are some within the Calvinist school of thought who are not satisfied with the way the problem of evil is handled as described above. This group, who are in the minority, is called hyper-Calvinists or hard determinists. They view their fellow Calvinists as not strong enough in their emphasis on God's governance or sovereignty on the issue of evil.

To the hyper-Calvinists or hard determinists, God is sovereign and does not have to rely on the distinction between ultimate cause and proximate cause to distinguish his actions from those of his creatures. To do so actually diminishes his sovereignty over evil. God can do whatever he wants to do as the governor of the world. Everything—including evil events—in the world comes about because of him. Thus, those who hold this view do not feel compelled to justify God's involvement with evil, since it is assumed that his ways are always right and good. It should be noted, though, that this variant of Calvinism is not representative of mainstream Calvinism when it comes to the problem of evil.

2. Grudem, *Systematic Theology*, 323.
3. Grudem, *Systematic Theology*, 323.
4. Grudem, *Systematic Theology*, 328.

The Arminian School of Thought on the Problem of Evil

On the problem of evil, the Arminian position is very straightforward. God has nothing directly to do with evil in the world, since he has given free will to human beings who can misuse it. And, because human beings do misuse it, evil must spring from human or creaturely free acts. To Calvinists, this approach does not go deep enough in accounting for the relationship of God and evil. What do we do with passages in the Bible where God asserts his sovereign control over evil or evil outcomes?

Looking at the simple approach of Arminians when it comes to the problem of evil, we are tempted to conclude that their position is different from that of Calvinists. But, interestingly, for all their dissimilarities, the Arminian and Calvinist positions have core similarities. We examine two key similarities.

First, both refuse to taint the holiness of God with any suggestion of evil (though they may differ on how this is done within their system). Second, both continue to uphold the sovereignty of God even in the face of evil. Like Calvinism, traditional Arminianism does not want to say that God's sovereignty has been diminished in any way when faced with evil. Evil is able to make its mark in the world only because God permits it to do so. It is on this second point of similarity with Calvinism that some within the Arminian school of thought have accused their fellow Arminians of inconsistency in their commitment to creaturely free will and have continued to hold on to Calvinistic notions of divine sovereignty. This group, which we encountered earlier, is known as Open Theists.

When it comes to the problem of evil, Open Theism wants Arminianism to be more distinct from Calvinism. It does not think that Arminians have taken seriously the free will that God has given creatures. Following the analysis of Richard Rice on foreknowledge, some Open Theists, such as Greg Boyd and Thomas Oord, want to employ the biblical metaphor of "warfare" or "spiritual warfare" to depict God's relationship with evil and to redefine what it means for God to give free will to evil spiritual creatures. They argue that we are to see God as locked in a spiritual battle with Satan and his forces, which have played a large role in wreaking havoc in human existence since time immemorial. God has given free will not only to humans but also to spirit beings like Satan and his angels. And their misuse of their free will is also what explains the suprahuman kinds of evil we see in the world today.

Open Theists argue that Arminians, like Calvinists, have sometimes mistakenly construed God's relationship with Satan and his minions as a master-servant relationship, since God is sovereign over them. They are seen as subservient agents of God who inevitably do his bidding for the ultimate good of humanity. So, evil or negative events that come our way—such as sickness or accidents—are viewed as sent from God when instead they should be viewed as the dastardly deeds of Satan and his minions. God's relationship with Satan, then, is not in any sense of the word cooperative in nature but rather is truly adversarial. Satan and his minions are bent on undermining God's purposes. And humans live in the midst of this spiritual warfare and suffer the consequences of it. This is, therefore, why evil happens in the world according to Open Theists. Failure to grasp this spiritual warfare blinds us from seeing evil for what it really is and causes us to mistakenly attribute negative events that come our way as somehow from God when they really are the works of the enemy of our souls.

To Open Theists, there is a strict separation of good and evil, the former coming from God and the latter from Satan. Failure to make this clear-cut distinction, they would say, leads to the irreverent attribution of evil to God. Moreover, it also fails to take into account the reality of spiritual warfare that Scripture describes human existence to be in. They accuse their Arminian brethren who have not taken the direction of Open Theism of becoming more like Calvinists when addressing the problem of evil.

No doubt, by emphasizing that evil results from spiritual warfare, the Open Theist approach makes very clear that there is no nexus between God and evil in the world. But this approach, when taken to its logical conclusion, suffers from an unfortunate side effect. It raises the specter of a dualistic concept of God. Note that there is a realm or force that brings about good in our world. He is God. And there is a realm or force that brings about evil in our world. He is Satan. The Bible, however, rejects this notion of seeming ontological dualism.

On this charge, Open Theists like Boyd and Oord would assert that God merely volunteered to withhold or limit his sovereign power to allow Satan and his angels to engage him in spiritual warfare.[5] In other words,

5. Boyd, *Satan and the Problem of Evil*; Oord, *Uncontrolling Love of God*.

Satan is not the ontological equal of God. This formal qualifying explanation may get Open Theists the seal of orthodoxy, but in practice, their consistent appeal to the limitations of God—both in terms of foreknowledge and omnipotence—certainly raises the question of whether they are truly doing Christian theology. One's theological emphasis on the doctrine of providence cannot help but color the mood and the portrayal of God as depicted in the Bible. While Open Theists may not formally subscribe to a full-blown dualism, a casual observer could easily mistake them for doing so in practice.

Recent Critique of Both the Calvinist and Arminian Positions on the Problem of Evil

"Theodicy" is the technical term for the theological discipline that seeks to justify or defend God's ways in the face of evil. What we have seen above are theodicies coming from Calvinism and Arminianism. Both are valiant efforts to provide a rational response to the problem of evil. Although they come from different perspectives—one utilizing a strong view of divine sovereignty, the other strongly emphasizing human free will—both are appealing to a cognitive or intellectual answer to the problem of evil. There is definitely a place for such a theological work.

However, as many theologians themselves have recently observed and complained, theodicy has eclipsed the need for a real, practical, and pastoral response to the problem of evil for the benefit of lay people.[6] In other words, when it comes to the problem of evil, the current state of the doctrine of providence is tilted toward debating the issues that theologians themselves want to pursue rather than focusing on the ways the laity might benefit from the doctrine. Therefore, for lay people to reap the benefits of what theologians are saying, the laity would almost have to become professional theologians themselves to enter the debate. But this current situation is problematic because it has made the doctrine of providence not only inaccessible to lay people but also irrelevant to them

6. See Tilley, *Evils of Theodicy*; Swinton, *Raging with Compassion*. Alvin Plantinga and John Feinberg make a distinction that seeks to create a different discussion of the problem of evil that can address the problems of the laity. This is a recognition that the current approach lacks the ability to address the practical concerns while it seeks to address the theological or theoretical. There has been, in short, a divorce.

because the issues that theologians raise, while intellectually important, are not of immediate and existential significance to the layperson. This is what James Daane means when he mentions that there is a "kind of theological intellectualism that passes for authentic theology and theological training in both evangelical and liberal seminaries."[7]

For there to be a proper revival of the doctrine of providence, we must not neglect the debates concerning the intellectual issues. But we must also trailblaze a new path in the doctrine of providence that would render it more accessible and, most of all, existentially relevant to lay people. This move is the need of the hour if we are to revitalize the doctrine of providence among the laity. When we do this, it might just cause the laity to value and appreciate the current theological debates while they reap the immediate existential benefits that the doctrine of providence gives them.

Reframing the Doctrine of Providence

As one can quickly see, the doctrine of providence in its current state is something of a conundrum for a typical layperson. Someone who wants to live purposefully and boldly, such as Sam Polk, the former Wall Street multimillionaire who turned to nonprofit work (see chap. 1), probably would not bother to settle the issues raised by Calvinism, Arminianism, or any other school of thought in Christianity. Such a person would likely end up attributing life's provisions to an ambiguous but simpler concept of "the universe" rather than to the personal God of providence found in Christianity.

It is high time, therefore, to reframe the doctrine of providence in an effort to transcend the theological debates and recover its intended existential impact regardless of what school of thought one may belong to. But how do we do this? I propose that we allow the grand narrative, or metanarrative, of Scripture to remake the way we theologize, relying on its way of looking at the world, instead of the influences around us.

The metanarrative of the Bible on which all Christian theology rests can be summarized in the following manner: creation, fall, redemption, and new creation.

7. Daane, "Respect for Theology," 89.

- *Creation* describes how God created the world and, in particular, humankind for his unique purpose.
- *Fall* refers to that event when humanity (starting with Adam and Eve in the garden of Eden) rebelled against God and set the trajectory of the whole human race in the direction of disobedience toward God, manifesting itself in the many human woes in society today.
- *Redemption* depicts God's relentless love, which led him to rescue fallen humanity from itself by setting into motion the plan of salvation that began with the calling of Abraham and his descendants, Israel, and culminates in the coming of the Messiah, Jesus Christ, to bring humanity back to the proper relationship that God intended for humankind in creation.
- *New creation* informs us that God is not done in bestowing his blessing upon humanity, since his plan of salvation includes, in the future, a new and better world without the presence of sin and with his presence fully manifested, which has always been the desire of every human soul.

This then, in a nutshell, is the basic storyline of the Bible that finds unanimous support from among Christian theological traditions that draw from Scripture their understanding of divine revelation on what constitutes reality and truth.

Although the biblical metanarrative is a story, it is not without propositional content. Indeed, if one were matching this basic storyline to the oldest creed of the church, the Apostles' Creed, it would correspond roughly in the following way:

- Article 1 deals with creation,
- Article 2 deals with fall and redemption, and
- Article 3 deals with new creation.

But we note again that it is this metanarrative from the Bible that feeds and informs how we formulate theological propositions that reflect the canonical whole of the scriptural message.

Thus, by returning to and reliving the metanarrative of Scripture, we allow the theological system of our mind to be "rebooted" according to

Metanarrative of the Bible	The Apostles' Creed (basic propositional truths of Christian theology)
Creation	**Article 1** I believe in God, the Father almighty, the Maker of heaven and earth,
Fall Redemption	**Article 2** and in Jesus Christ, his only Son, our Lord, who was conceived by the Holy Spirit, born of the Virgin Mary, suffered under Pontius Pilate, was crucified, died and was buried; he descended into hell; on the third day he rose again from the dead; he ascended into heaven, and is seated at the right hand of God the Father almighty; from there he will come to judge the living and the dead.
New Creation	**Article 3** I believe in the Holy Spirit, the holy catholic Church, the communion of saints, the forgiveness of sins, the resurrection of the body, and life everlasting. Amen.

the theodrama of Scripture as we do theology. Or to use a more biblical term, we allow the metanarrative to "renew" our minds (Rom. 12:2). Like a nearsighted person who gains focus with a pair of eyeglasses, we gain a clearer perspective or feel on how to "image" or "reimage" a difficult theological issue. And it just might provide a clarifying theological breakthrough in light of the story of the Bible as a whole. This is what I mean in this book by framing providence in view of the seventh and eighth days of creation. Such an approach is centered on the storyline of Scripture's metanarrative.

Narratives have a way of helping us recalibrate our ability to perceive a theological issue better than straightforward propositional statements of theology can do. Perhaps this is why the Bible itself is not organized like a textbook with an encyclopedic index geared to different topics, but rather tells a grand story that draws us in to experience the divine author's perspective of what reality is. It is from here (encountering the divine author's words set to the narrative key) that we are to theologize and address issues such as providence in a propositional way.

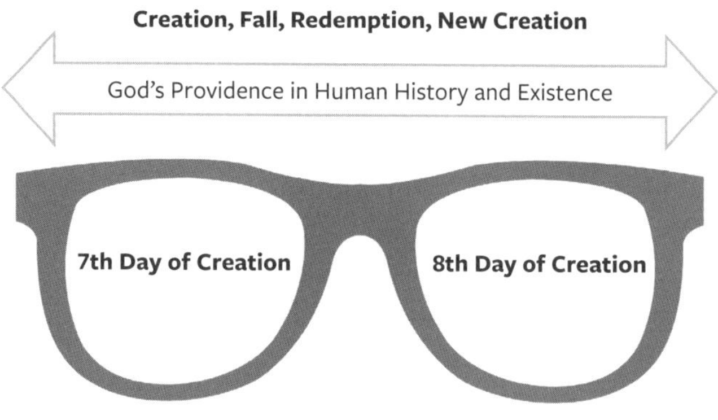

Figure 2.4

Kevin Vanhoozer elaborates on how the theological process should properly work going from the Bible's metanarrative to theological propositional statements. First, he astutely observes,

> Narratives (to continue with this example) actually do more than *display the world*. They also establish a point of view: the stance of the narrator. . . . Stories do not simply relate a sequence of events but also suggest, sometimes explicitly and sometimes implicitly, how one should *take* the description: the stance of the narrator. . . . In writing narratives and thus *displaying a world*, then, authors indirectly communicate a *world view* as well.[8]

This impartation of a worldview then enables us to do theology from a narrative whole that is often missing for many Christians who attempt to theologize today.

Second, Vanhoozer states, "By inculcating a worldview, narrative is far more than a way of transmitting information; it is rather a process of *formation*: a training in *seeing as*. . . . And not only seeing. The imagination is the bearer of modes of seeing, experiencing, being."[9] Thus, "a 'biblical' theology, therefore, involves more than summarizing the propositional content of the Scriptures. It involves acquiring cognitive skills and sensibilities, and hence *the ability to see, feel and taste the world as disclosed in the diverse biblical texts*."[10]

8. Vanhoozer, *Drama of Doctrine*, 284.
9. Vanhoozer, *Drama of Doctrine*, 284.
10. Vanhoozer, *Drama of Doctrine*, 285.

Third, this narrative approach in addressing the doctrine of providence does not involve forsaking completely our reliance on propositional truths in doing systematic theology. Rather, it means that "we must go beyond propositional revelation" but "we must take propositions with us."[11]

Put another way, using Charles Taylor's terminology, the biblical metanarrative of creation, fall, redemption, and new creation is the Christians' "social imaginary" from which they theologize, frame reality, and live life. The more one returns to this foundational social imaginary, the more one is able to view issues closer and closer to the Christian point of view. It doesn't mean, of course, that one is able to finally reach a perfect articulation of the Christian position on a given issue. But it will be, at least, a faithful articulation that one can continue to refine using the same method.

What follows, then, is this book's attempt to return to the biblical metanarrative in order to bring about a cohesive theological framework for the currently fragmented and overly abstract doctrine of God's providence. In using this methodology, it aims to make the doctrine of providence graspable, memorable, and inhabitable. Practically speaking, the book envisions how best to communicate the doctrine of providence to someone, such as Sam Polk or Terry Waite, who desperately needs the immediate benefit of the doctrine of providence without getting bogged down in the theological niceties that often plague its usage.

11. Vanhoozer, *Drama of Doctrine*, 278.

3

God's Providence in the Pre-Fall Seventh Day of Creation

> People say that what we're all seeking is a meaning for life. I don't think that's what we're really seeking. I think that what we're seeking is an experience of being alive, so that our life experiences on the purely physical plane will have resonances with our own innermost being and reality, so that we actually feel the rapture of being alive.
>
> —Joseph Campbell, *The Power of Myth*

Heightening the Relevance of Providence through Vocation

In Harvey Cox's seminal work, *The Secular City*, he makes an important observation about God and modern humanity. "The word *God*," he says, "means almost nothing to modern secular man. His mental world and his way of using language is such that he can neither understand nor use the word *God* meaningfully."[1] Why is that? Using a different terminology but the same concept that Charles Taylor uses, Cox points to the change in our society's social imaginary as the reason for our inability to properly perceive God and, thus, providence. He writes,

1. Cox, *Secular City*, 241.

> To name is to point, to confess, to locate something in terms of our history. We can name something only by using the fund of memories and meanings we carry with us as individuals and as a species. This makes the act of naming, whether naming God or anything else, more than merely a theological or linguistic problem. Theologies and languages grow out of a sociocultural milieu.[2]

But ours is an age when God is no longer seen as necessary because humanity now lives in a sophisticated world where technology can seemingly meet all our needs. So to say "God"—as the Bible portrays him to be—no longer evokes in us the same mental image and the same visceral reaction that it did for our forebears.

Given this situation, how should we speak of God in our self-sufficient society today? Cox suggests that the proper context to meaningfully convey God today is to portray him as someone who comes alongside humanity in their work situation or life-chore relatedness. He explains that in our "peculiar urban" society, we are conditioned to see an authentic relationship as one that revolves around "work" or the fulfilling of a "life chore," since we spend so much time every day in it. Indeed, both our existence and self-identity depend on it. So, anyone who contributes to this essential, daily existential routine is a candidate for someone with whom we can develop a deep, authentic relationship of dependence. The reason this observation is crucial, according to Cox, is that this way of perceiving what constitutes an authentic relationship is "bound to influence our symbolization of God in one way or another."[3] Thus, if theologians can adapt this teamwork metaphor to express the mutuality that God wants to have with us, then secular humankind might just be able to apprehend more easily the relevance of God and his providence in their life.

Cox's communication approach has a lot to be commended. It is unmistakable that our world is becoming more and more centered on "work" or the work motif of living. Even the "immanent frame" that Charles Taylor referred to as the driving force behind our current secular age is "immanent" only insofar as it is a reality produced by the effort of human work or humans working together. Thus, in agreement with Cox, I see the need to communicate the doctrine of providence to modern humankind in the

2. Cox, *Secular City*, 242.
3. Cox, *Secular City*, 264.

context of work. But, while agreeing, I make some key qualifications and modifications to his suggested theological approach.

First, the emphasis on communicating theology through the language of work is not "new" and certainly not "unprecedented" as Cox depicts it to be. It is rather old and can be found in the very first pages of the Bible. Genesis speaks of how God created humanity to work by exercising dominion on earth as his regents. This is clearly seen when humanity gives names to the animals and tends the garden of Eden. So, the theological methodology that Cox helpfully stresses is but a recovery of an ancient insight. It is, in short, a thoroughly biblical approach.

Second, not only is the approach of communicating providence via work an old one, but also it actually has a narrative or a story (an etiology) connected to it in the Bible. It behooves us, therefore, to revisit and rehearse this story if we are to properly understand the doctrine of providence through the lens of work that lies at the heart of human existence. Rather than speaking in generalities or pure proposition, Christian theology is best done in the context of human vocation, which brings out the full relevance of the doctrine of providence to theologians and laity alike. For such an approach, to use Cox's phrase, "is bound to influence our symbolization of God."

The Six-Day Creation Account

The first act of the metanarrative found in the Bible is creation. In the beginning is the God who has no beginning. He did not create because he was lonely and needed companionship or anything else from what he might create. For his divine life—made up of the eternal mutual love of Father, Son, and Holy Spirit—is self-sustaining and, therefore, does not suffer any want. Indeed, creation springs forth from the overflow of God's inner life of love.

In a well-ordered and measured manner, he created all that there is in this world in six days of divine work,[4] producing material and immaterial things, visible and invisible realms, animal and plant kingdoms—everything that

4. Some see the six-day creation as literal twenty-four-hour days, while others see them as a long period of time. This chapter does not intend to get into the discussion but only to state that, regardless of one's view, the point of the Genesis account is to demonstrate that God created in a purposeful and ordered fashion. Moreover, regardless of one's theory of the exact nature

is a part of our reality today. Finally, he created humanity as the "jewel" of his creation because he made us in his own image.

So unique is this way of creating the world that theologians coined a term to capture its essence: *creatio ex nihilo* ("creation out of nothing"). But, regardless of terminology, what is put on display in this vast canvas of the creation account found in Genesis and elsewhere in the Bible is not only his power but also his goodness and wisdom in creating all that there is. But more than that, we are to see creation and ourselves as the outward manifestation of the love that is inherent in the core of his divine being.

How God created humanity receives special attention in Scripture. The Bible emphasizes the special touch that God gives to the creation of humanity. God created the first man by picking up a lump of clay and molding and shaping it. Then, he breathed his breath into that lump of clay, which became a living being.

What makes this creation of humanity unique is not just that God was meticulous in his way of creating us but also the intimacy involved when he infused something of himself (his breath) into the being of man. Thus, it connotes the idea that, in creating man, God imparted to him something very special of himself. Nowhere in the Bible's creation account do we see other creatures given the same dignity of this divine personal touch.

Later, when man (Adam) in the garden needed human companionship, God took notice of it and acted on his behalf. While Adam was asleep, he took a rib from Adam's side and created a companion out of it. This shows that God gave Adam a companion who is of equal importance and possesses equal dignity. Thus, in the creation account of both genders of humankind, God conveys a very special role and place that he has for them in the created order. That special purpose is bound up in the rather enigmatic but repeated phrase in Genesis, that humanity is made in God's image.

The Meaning of the *Imago Dei*

In Genesis 1:26, God says, "Let Us make man in Our image, according to Our likeness." But what does that mean? There are two senses to what

of how God created the world, the point I am making here stands, since it centers not on other species in God's creation but on the purpose of the creation of humankind.

it means for God to make us in his own image. While distinct from each other, these two senses are really complementary in nature.

The first meaning of the image of God in humankind is that God created humans with qualities or attributes that are similar to his own attributes. Granted that we do not possess all of God's attributes; nonetheless, we do have the same attributes that he has, such as the ability to love, to think, to feel, to be sociable, and so on (commonly known in theology as communicable attributes). It is here in Genesis 2's account of God breathing his breath into humanity that we have a graphic account of this transference of divine attributes to humanity. Thus, with this image of God in humanity, it can be said that humans are more similar to God in attributes than any of God's other created things. Often, this is how most people understand what the *imago Dei* is. But the term is loaded with meaning, so we must turn to its other sense if we are to do justice to it.

The second meaning of the image of God in humankind is that God created humanity with a function or task similar to his own. The passages in Genesis that discuss God's image in humanity do not appear in isolation but rather are connected to the purpose for which it was given to humanity. So, in Genesis 1:26, after saying, "Let Us make man in Our image, according to Our likeness," God goes on to make clear his reason: "and let them rule over the fish of the sea and over the birds of the sky and over the cattle and over all the earth, and over every creeping thing that creeps on the earth." To further underscore this rationale, God repeats it in his command in verse 28: "Be fruitful and multiply, and fill the earth, and subdue it; and rule over the fish of the sea and over the birds of the sky and over every living thing that moves on the earth." Just like God is ruler of creation, humanity is also designated to be corulers with God in creation.

Interestingly, the phrase "image of God" has an ancient connotation that most of the original readers (or listeners, to be more precise) of Genesis would have immediately recognized. But they would also detect a twist in the usage of the term. In the ancient Near East, kings are said to possess the "image of God" as they are designated on earth to rule on God's behalf. But going against the conventional usage of the term at that time, Genesis does not confer this designation of being made in the image of God merely to human kings but rather to all of humanity (descendants of

Adam and Eve). Later, the psalmist, in Psalm 8, confirms this egalitarian and universal understanding of the *imago Dei* on all humans with the following poetic description:

> What is man that You take thought of him,
> And the son of man that You care for him?
> Yet You have made him a little lower than God,
> And You crown him with glory and majesty!
> You make him to rule over the works of Your hands;
> You have put all things under his feet,
> All sheep and oxen,
> And also the beasts of the field,
> The birds of the heavens and the fish of the sea,
> Whatever passes through the paths of the seas. (Ps. 8:4–8)

In view of this unique teaching of the Bible on the image of God in man, Gerhard von Rad clarifies the functional sense of the *imago Dei* this way:

> Just as powerful earthly kings, to indicate their claim to dominion, erect an image of themselves in the provinces of their empire where they do not personally appear, so man is placed upon earth in God's image as God's sovereign emblem. He is really only God's representative, summoned to maintain and enforce God's claim to dominion over the earth.[5]

There is no mistaking that the image of God in humanity is, indeed, a unique teaching in the Bible when compared to its ancient usage.

To be made in the image of God in this functional sense, therefore, is not simply a matter of ontology (the human makeup) but also a matter of responsibility (the human task). This is why the two senses of the *imago Dei* are not mutually exclusive but are complementary to each other. As a matter of observation, we tend to forget the responsibility part of the *imago Dei* and, often, simply dwell on the dignity part of the term. But, it is the former sense that brings out the active and purposive connotation of the image of God in humanity. It therefore lays out the divine telos or program for human existence. It directs us to be about the business of being God's corulers in this world.

5. Von Rad, *Genesis*, 60.

The Seventh Day of Creation

The creation account in Genesis concludes with a rather jarring description of what God did next, on the seventh day of creation:

> By the seventh day God completed His work which He had done, and He rested on the seventh day from all His work which He had done. Then God blessed the seventh day and sanctified it, because in it He rested from all His work which God had created and made. (Gen. 2:2)

Rest? Why? Surely, it is not that he became tired and weary, for we have already established that he is self-sufficient and all-powerful. It is in the unpacking of the meaning of this divine rest, which God sanctified, that we discover the deeper meaning of our human existence. Indeed, it is in this divine "rest" that we understand how the rest of the human story unfolds. I offer three ways to view the significance of God's "rest" in the biblical metanarrative as it relates to the doctrine of providence.

Active Human Participation in Creation Care

By resting from his wondrous activity of *creatio ex nihilo*, God allowed humanity to have a meaningful role in creation. Imagine God resuming his awe-inspiring work of creation. Consider further if there had been no seventh day of divine rest. Such continuing divine activity would have left humanity awestruck and unable to do what God intended for humanity to do. For the human tendency is to defer to such magnificent power at work. But by resting on the seventh day of creation, God made possible for humans to now act as his corulers in this world, thus confirming the functional view of the *imago Dei*. God's act of deferring to humanity by "resting" from creating has led theologians like Luther and other medieval theologians to describe God's present involvement in the world as *Deus absconditus* (the hiddenness of God).[6] It is a term not of derision but of acknowledgment that God has given a measure of autonomy to humanity. On the seventh day of creation, the *Deus faber* (God the creator) deliberately made space for his *homo faber* (human worker) to operate as his *imago Dei*.

This understanding is further confirmed by the way Adam and Eve are portrayed in Genesis as "naming" the animals. This activity involves

6. See Walton, *Genesis*, 146–57.

studying and overseeing the animal kingdom well enough to "name" them (Gen. 2:19–20). And they are also depicted as "cultivating" the garden of Eden (Gen. 2:15). Land cultivation involves agriculture and, thus, mastery of the plant kingdom. In both instances it is evident that God did not create a completed world (which he could have done) such that humanity has nothing more to add to it. Rather, God created a world in which Adam and Eve have a role to contribute to its further development. It is this contribution of humanity that God's rest has made possible. John Stott gives this helpful word of clarification:

> We need, then, to make an important distinction between nature and culture. Nature is what God gives us; culture is what we make of it (agriculture, horticulture, etc.). Nature is raw materials; culture is commodities prepared for the market. Nature is divine creation; culture is human cultivation. God invites us to share in his work. Indeed, our work becomes a privilege when we see it as collaboration with God.[7]

Interestingly, though, that same rest of God that made possible the human ability to live out their calling has also made possible the ability to spurn that calling. As God himself told Adam and Eve, they have the ability to obey God's command not to eat of the tree of the knowledge of good and evil or to disobey it and suffer its consequences. Paradoxically, this is what the rest of God on the seventh day has also made possible.

On the seventh day of creation, then, God gave humanity the gift of freedom or free will to be or not to be the divine image bearers that he created them to be. God's rest entailed the participation of human choices in creation. This is the dignity God has conferred upon human beings. But, as we will see later, there are certain parameters to this human freedom or free will that we must also take into account if we are to accurately understand it from a biblical point of view.

Recognition of Mortal Limitation in the Human Task

The seventh-day creation "rest" of God is also intended to teach humankind of their human limitation as exemplified by God himself. Human

7. Stott, *Through the Bible*, 23.

beings are mortal creatures. We have a physical limitation on how much we can work. We cannot engage in ceaseless activity in life. Thus, God's rest shows us the pattern of how humans are to work and rest. As God himself demonstrates in the creation account of Genesis, humans are to work six days, but then they are to rest one day, a day of Sabbath rest. This workweek cycle is for their well-being. Later in the Pentateuch, God makes even clearer his rationale for the seventh day of rest. In Deuteronomy 5:13–15, God commands,

> Six days you shall labor and do all your work, but the seventh day is a sabbath of the Lord your God; in it you shall not do any work . . . so that your male servant and your female servant may rest as well as you. You shall remember that you were a slave in the land of Egypt, and the Lord your God brought you out of there by a mighty hand and by an outstretched arm; therefore the Lord your God commanded you to observe the sabbath day.

In this divine "rest" we are reminded of our mortality and that we are not machines that can work 24/7 nonstop. For if God himself, who needs no rest, rested, how much more should we?

While the seventh-day rest of God reminds us of our physical need to rest, it also points us to the fact that we are beings with a mental and emotional capacity that needs regular refreshing. That aspect of our human existence must also be nurtured in the manner that God himself exemplified. God rested at the end of each "day" of his creation by pausing to marvel at the "goodness" of what he created. And at the end of his entire six-day creation, Genesis 1:31 tells us, "God saw all that He had made, and behold, it was very good. And there was evening and there was morning, the sixth day." When God rested, he took in the beauty and the goodness of his creation. He saw that it was good and, indeed, very good. This too is part of what it means for us to rest: aesthetics, enjoying the intangibles of God's creation and what God has called us to do. Certainly, this is one of the ways God is conveying to us how we are to rest for the benefit of our human existence. Physical rest without the rest of the human soul is incomplete.

We must cease from our work temporarily to enjoy the fruits of our labor. Without this kind of rest envisioned by God on the seventh day of creation, our life will be imbalanced. How good God is to demonstrate this deeper aspect of our rest for us on the seventh day of creation! For this too is a very wise and loving provision he has given to humanity.

How strictly must this ceasing from work be observed? Certainly, in the time of Jesus this was a hotly debated issue. In their zeal to observe the Sabbath, the Pharisees came up with many rules on what constitutes physical stoppage of work. But they missed the whole point of the Sabbath and did not go deep enough into the true intent of the Sabbath teaching. For the rest that God wants humanity to experience is not just physical rest but also soul rest. As psychosomatic creatures, we must attend to both body and mind, just as God demonstrated in the creation account. The mistake of the Pharisees is that they focused on the physical nature of rest alone.

Whatever refreshes and builds up our soul is also the "rest" God envisioned for humanity on the Sabbath observance. This is, no doubt, what Jesus meant when he said, "The Sabbath was made for man, and not man for the Sabbath" (Mark 2:27). No wonder Jesus observed the Sabbath in a dynamic, nonlegalistic way, seeking to "do good" on that day because such an activity is consistent with God's intent of producing "soul rest" for humanity on the Sabbath day (see Mark 3:1–5).

There is, then, a complementary relationship between the rest of the outer man and the rest of the inner man that the Sabbath is teaching us. We do not desist from physical work for its own sake on the Sabbath day. Rather, we do so in order that our soul might also be strengthened and might be able to pursue what God has called us to do. Often, our physical rest is what paves the way for us to engage in the deeper aspect of soul rest. Maintaining this complementary nature of rest fulfills the kind of rest that God wants to give humanity in order that humankind might function properly as his image bearers in creation.

When we observe this Sabbath principle properly as seen in the seventh day of creation, the benefit of inner rejuvenating and reinvigorating joy that God promised in Isaiah 58:13–14 becomes his divine provision for us in a very real way:

> If you keep your feet from breaking the Sabbath
>   and from doing as you please on my holy day,
> if you call the Sabbath a delight
>   and the Lord's holy day honorable,

and if you honor it by not going your own way
and not doing as you please or speaking idle words,
then you will find your joy in the LORD,
and I will cause you to ride in triumph on the heights of the land
and to feast on the inheritance of your father Jacob. (NIV)

Living in Dependent Partnership with God

Despite making room for humanity to play a significant role in his completed creation, God is not an absentee landlord who leaves humanity to run the field of creation like tenants without a supervisor. For, as Jesus said, God is ever working. The seventh-day rest of God pertains only to abstaining from his work of original creation (see John 5:16–18). Thus, while humanity works, God is also working in their midst, sustaining them, guiding them, ruling them, and even overruling them. If God is, indeed, an active and integral being in the world, then it behooves humanity to befriend him if we are to truly understand who we are, what we are to do, and how to find meaning in our earthly existence. And the seventh day of creation is God's heuristic device to impress upon us that reality.

The seventh day of creation points us beyond our own personal need of physical and soul rest toward something even deeper: the rest that comes from our communion with God. In this time of communion with him, an inexplicable deep yearning within us is satisfied. It is, as the psalmist said, deep calling to deep (Ps. 42:7). Such a time of communion results in having our internal queries addressed in either expressible or inexpressible ways. But, in either case, we come away from the time of communion with God with a sense of completeness and direction to once again carry on God's given task to be his image bearers in the world. In this way of looking at humanity, we affirm that humans are more than just *homo faber* (human worker); they are also *homo adorans* (human worshiper, worshiping humanity).

There are some who might wonder if Sabbath was observed in the garden of Eden or if the reference to Sabbath in Genesis is merely foreshadowing what Israel would later formally observe as a nation. Scholars debate over this issue, for which there is no final resolution. Certainly, nothing in Genesis tells us of when or how the first Sabbath was observed as a formal religious event.

However, if in the meaning of the term "Sabbath" we include the generic idea of setting aside time to rest from work and to commune with God, then it is easy to establish that this informal sense of observing Sabbath happened in the garden of Eden. For Genesis records that part of the pre-fall human existence in the garden included Adam and Eve communing regularly with God (Gen. 3:8). Such a meeting would naturally involve ceasing from work and interacting with God. We are not told how often this meeting occurred. Certainly, it was regular enough that Adam and Eve were not surprised that God came looking for them after they ate from the forbidden tree and hid themselves. It would not be too farfetched to believe that the meeting took place on the Sabbath day. But, regardless, there was a definite time set aside from work in order to interact with God—an informal Sabbath observance.

This regular turning to God in order to commune with him was the habitual practice of Adam and Eve in the garden of Eden. No doubt this is an inference, but it is a very probable activity. We do not know exactly the nature of their meeting with God in the cool of the day. It is safe to assume that the topic of their communion conversation would, at least, cover what transpired in their experiences in the garden. And from there, they would not only share their observations but also derive from God the insights necessary to live as God would have them do.

The picture we get, therefore, of pre-fall human existence is that, while humanity was in the midst of doing their God-given task in the garden, humankind did so in constant, regular consultation with him. And this "rest" as represented by the seventh day of creation was done not in a mechanical or legalistic fashion but rather in the context of a spontaneous, joyful communion with God. So, the true balanced human existence as depicted in the garden of Eden includes this important element of "rest" in the form of communion with God so that the *imago Dei* can be properly discharged in and through humanity.

Such moments of "rest" through communion with God not only soothe the human soul but also impart the knowledge necessary to fulfill humanity's God-given task. This is seen especially in relation to the tree of the knowledge of good and evil. When God prohibited Adam and Eve from partaking of it, the interesting question of whether Adam and Eve already possessed the knowledge of good and evil arises. One might be inclined to assume that they did. After all, didn't we establish that humanity was created in the image of God, which presumably would include such a knowledge? But if so, why would Adam and Eve desire something that they already possessed? For that matter, why would it be a temptation later for the serpent to dangle this knowledge of good and evil in front of them if they already have it? The best response is to say that there was a modicum of the knowledge of good and evil already inherent in humankind through the God-imparted *imago Dei*. We would even add that humanity has the mental capacity to understand the meaning of ethically right and ethically wrong. But, like the other communicable attributes of God given to humanity, this knowledge of good and evil is not exhaustive or all-encompassing. In other words, it needs supplementation and further development.

Although humanity may have the rational capacity to understand what is right and what is wrong, they were not given the ability or authority to independently decide for themselves what constitutes good and evil. Such a determination lies with God alone. So, humanity must always look to God and, indeed, must develop within themselves an attitude of constant reliance on him for the determination of what is good and what is evil. And this is the point of the seventh day of creation. God has designed human existence to be incomplete without him. The seventh day of creation is a heuristic device to help us remember this existential reality and to live in light of it. As Ray Anderson eloquently puts it,

> Human freedom is not a freedom *from* that which binds the self, but a freedom *for* that which determines the self. Adam and Eve experienced themselves in a freedom of fellowship and response to the very source of their creaturely life—the Lord God. . . . This is the biblical concept of freedom: not to be determined by the creature of the sixth day, but to be drawn into the seventh day by a determination which is experienced as a creaturely life . . . oriented toward fellowship and participation in the life of God.[8]

With this relationship of dependence in mind, a helpful metaphor emerges for the relationship of human existence and divine providence. What is being conveyed is a picture of a partnership that God is allowing humanity to have with him in creation. When we think of a partnership, we often think of a fifty-fifty setup whereby each partner has equal say. But this was not the kind of partnership that God envisioned when he created humanity within the framework of the seventh day of creation.

8. Anderson, *On Being Human*, 78–79.

In the business and legal world, there are various kinds of partnerships to choose from when forming such a relationship. The "limited partnership" model captures well the kind of partnership that God wanted to have with humanity when he created them. Granted, this "limited partnership" analogy is anachronistic, but it serves as a clarifying metaphor and illustrates well the divine-human partnership that the seventh day of creation depicts.

A "limited partnership" is a type of business arrangement whereby the business entity is made up of two types of partners: the general partner and the limited partner. The general partner operates the day-to-day affairs of the business, while the limited partner provides the capital resources necessary for the business to operate. The limited partner is a "silent" partner in granting the general partner discretion to make business operational decisions. The general partner, though in the forefront of the company, is still accountable to the limited partner. Indeed, the general partner would be wise to work in close conjunction with the limited partner, whose resources and advice the general partner needs.

In this way of understanding partnership, one can quickly see how a limited partnership serves as a good analogy or metaphor for the relationship of human existence and divine providence. Humanity is the general partner whom God, the limited partner, has given a great deal of discretion to run his business called creation. Not only did he start the business, but he also pledges to underwrite the business with all the necessary capital that his general partner needs to successfully operate their joint venture. Every time we come to our divine limited partner for advice and consent, we walk away with a greater ability and confidence to face the issues of living out the *imago Dei*. In him, therefore, we find our "rest" because, through our communion with him, all that we endeavor to do in life finds its provision and completion. The seventh day of creation, therefore, is designed to remind humanity of its dependent partnership with God and to beckon us to commune with our divine partner so that we might find our "rest" from the stresses of our labor.

Humanity (junior partner)	God (senior partner)
• Humanity, the junior partner, operates in the freedom and authority given it by God, the senior partner, to attend to the business of the created order. • Humanity, as the junior partner, regularly and deliberately turns to God for reliance, advice, and communion.	• God, the senior partner, faithfully underwrites everything the junior partner needs to care for the created order. • God, the wise and loving senior partner, ministers to the junior partner, caring for their well-being and restoring their weary soul.

Jesus: The Embodiment of the Pre-Fall Seventh Day of Creation Human Existence

The Genesis record of life in Eden gives us a glimpse of what humanity was like before the fall of humankind into sin and expulsion from the garden. One wishes, though, that we had more instances of how Adam and Eve lived out their humanity according to the *imago Dei*, especially as it relates to the seventh day of creation Sabbath principle discussed above. But anything we say about that pre-fall human existence would be pure speculation. We do, though, have something better to enlighten us about it. We have the life of Jesus Christ—the second and last Adam—recorded for us to look at and learn of God's original design. Jesus, who is God incarnate, is the embodiment of the seventh-day creation human existence before the fall.

In Jesus Christ, we see a man who freely and actively lived out his life for God and in partnership with him. Indeed, he lived his earthly life not so much from his own divine power and strength or even from his innate human power but in reliance on the power of the Spirit of God, who indwelled him. As active as he was, per the Gospel accounts, it was his regular custom or habit to withdraw from the crowd and spend time with God the Father in prayer. One could say that he often retired and found his rest in God. So, every day was his Sabbath day because every day he had his Sabbath moments with God.

He was not so much against the Jewish understanding that keeping the Sabbath involved refraining from physical work or activity. But he had a deeper and more dynamic way of understanding the Sabbath that transcended the Jewish understanding. Jesus aimed for the spirit of the Sabbath, not the letter of it. Sabbath day for him, no doubt, included physical rest, but it was not necessarily passive. It was a day sanctified or hallowed for God and his purposes, which meant, if need be, meeting the needs of others, thereby demonstrating God's reign over and concern for a creation that is suffering and fallen to sin.

Looking at Jesus, the second Adam, we see the human ideal of what God intended for humanity to be before the fall. In Jesus's case, he freely lived out God the Father's calling in his life (to be the Savior of the world). Jesus did this in reliance upon God's providence as exemplified by the seventh day of creation principle discussed above. This is what human existence is supposed to be. As the second-century church father Irenaeus rightly observed, "For the glory of God is a living man; and the life of man consists in beholding God."[9] But something happened to this ideal such that human existence is no longer an adventure lived in partnership with God.

9. Irenaeus, *Against Heresies* 4.20.7 (*ANF* 1:490).

4

God's Providence in the Post-Fall Seventh Day of Creation

> Don't you see the plants, the birds, the ants and spiders and bees going about their individual tasks, putting the world in order, as best they can?
>
> And you're not willing to do your job as a human being?
>
> Why aren't you running to do what your nature demands?
>
> —Marcus Aurelius, *Meditations*

When the Partnership Breaks Up

It's one of the biggest pizza chains in the world. But like many successful business enterprises, Domino's Pizza had a humble beginning. Two brothers, Tom and Jim Monaghan, entered into a business partnership in 1960. They borrowed $900 to buy a struggling pizzeria in Ypsilanti, Michigan, which eventually became Domino's Pizza. The gradual growth of Domino's Pizza soon demanded more and more of the brothers' time and energy, which tested their resolve to continue their fledgling business and, ultimately, their partnership.

In what now seems like an inexplicable move, Jim quit the partnership. No one knew for sure why he did it, except that the decision came as a surprise to many observers because the original idea of buying the pizza shop was his. Several possible reasons are given. Jim preferred to focus on his day job working at the postal service (which is more mellow and secure) rather than the hectic and financially risky life of restaurant entrepreneurship. Others believe that Jim disagreed with Tom's business decision to sell pizzas only. At that time, their restaurant also sold sandwiches and other fast foods. Still others believe that Jim did not want to play second fiddle to Tom, who was making all the major business decisions and seemingly having success in doing so. In that sense, he wanted to completely free himself from the shadow of his partner, Tom.

Regardless of the true reason, leaving the partnership turned out to be a huge business blunder. When Jim sold his half of Domino's Pizza to Tom, he gladly accepted as fair compensation a 1959 Volkswagen Beetle used for delivering pizza. Whatever the value of the car was, it certainly could not compare to what the 50 percent share turned out to be. In 1998, when Tom Monaghan sold Domino's Pizza, the company was worth one billion dollars. Had Jim stayed with the partnership, he could have gotten more than the value of a used Volkswagen Beetle.[1]

The story of humankind as portrayed in the Bible has a tragic similarity to the partnership of the Monaghan brothers. God conferred on humanity the extraordinary privilege of being his partners in the care of creation. But, similar to Jim Monaghan's decision, humanity inexplicably gave up on that partnership with God. Such a move, in effect, is what the Bible refers to as humanity's fall into sin. The difference, of course, is that disregarding or leaving our partnership with God brings much more severe consequences than the loss of financial profit. Another important difference is that, unlike the irredeemable broken partnership of the Monaghan brothers, God, our senior partner, continues to beckon humanity to return to his intended partnership with us and graciously provides us with the means to do so. These divine lifelines offered after humanity walked away from its partnership with God constitute what I call God's seventh-day providence post-fall. As we will see, though, despite humanity's stubborn refusal to return to the partnership, somehow God is still able to accomplish his goal of

1. Alexandra Cass, "The Truth about the Brothers Who Started Domino's," *Mashed*, April 27, 2021, https://www.mashed.com/393689/the-truth-about-the-brothers-who-started-dominos.

caring for creation through humanity's witting as well as unwitting cooperation with him.

One cannot fully understand or appreciate the biblical teaching of God's providence on the seventh day of creation without seriously taking into account the fall of humankind into sin. The gravity of this event is the proper context in which we are to understand the workings of divine providence in human existence. Thus, we take a brief overview of this important but tragic event before looking at specific ways God provides for humanity after the fall.

The Pursuit of the Knowledge of Good and Evil

The book of Genesis records the biblical account of the fall of humanity into sin for the first time. While a true historic event, it also serves as a paradigm for all subsequent human temptations and actions in which humanity continues to violate its partnership with God on an individual level. This event in Genesis, then, is an etiology—that is, an explanation of why humanity is in sin and continues to be in a sinful state. As such, therefore, it not only demonstrates why sin has such a vise grip on humanity but also, more importantly, emphasizes the necessity of God's providence in light of the human predicament.

In the lush greenery of the garden of Eden there existed a tree called the tree of the knowledge of good and evil (Gen. 2:9). God strongly warned Adam and Eve, our first parents, not to eat of its fruit lest they die (2:17), for the effect of doing so is that their "eyes will be opened" and that they "will be like God, knowing good and evil" (3:5). Amazingly, Adam and Eve succumbed to the temptation of the serpent (Satan) to eat from it so that they might be endowed with the knowledge of good and evil.

As stated in the previous chapter, however, a strong presumption can be made that Adam and Eve already possessed the basic ability to recognize good and evil by virtue of being made in the image of God. So why did the tree of the knowledge of good and evil still hold such an appeal to them that they were tempted by it? The reason must be that the tree offered something more than what they had before. To be precise, it imparted the kind of knowledge of good and evil that only God possessed. This understanding of the appeal is clearly attested to by both the serpent, who tempted them, and God, who warned them of the effects of eating from the tree (3:22).

But what is so bad about seeking to possess such a godlike knowledge? Why is death the consequence to Adam and Eve (or any human being for that matter) for obtaining such a godlike knowledge? A lot can be said on this matter. But the following serves as a succinct reason.

To eat from the tree of the knowledge of good and evil is tantamount to a deliberate breach of the existing partnership between God and humanity. Prior to eating from the tree, the way humanity would know more of what constituted good and evil was to receive it from God, their senior partner. He alone determined the makeup of good and evil. It is not hard to imagine how this impartation of knowledge would occur before the fall. As part of their partnership with God, Adam and Eve met and communed with God regularly in the cool of the day. It was the perfect time for the junior partners to seek the wisdom of their senior partner on how to properly discharge their creation mandate. Obviously, this would also involve any issues related to "good and evil."[2] This is the ideal relationship through which humanity may learn matters that are within God's prerogative alone. But to eat from the tree is to make a brash statement of self-emancipation from the humble state of dependence on God, thus violating the structure of partnership that God envisioned for humanity.

In other words, by eating from the tree of the knowledge of good and evil, humanity has arrogated to themselves decisions only God can make. Good and evil are now based on human self-determination. The Genesis narrative captured well what happened next to the human consciousness when it was emancipated from a state of God-dependence. After eating from the tree, "the eyes of both of them were opened" (Gen. 3:7). Independent of God, Adam and Eve became aware that they were naked. They deemed their nakedness something to be ashamed of, such that they sewed fig leaves to cover themselves before God. The issue here is not that they gained a new physical sight but rather a new psychological insight derived, unfortunately, from their own self-determination.

2. Walton, *Genesis*, 170–72, 214–17. Walton sees "good and evil" not in a narrow sense of ethical issues or decision-making issues but as a merism that includes all kinds of knowledge. I can go along with that, but I have chosen to narrow the matter to just the ethical, though I do not limit it to that.

What was opened to their eyes after they ate of the fruit is the question of what to do and how to deal with their nakedness: Is it something to be ashamed of or not? Is it proper or improper? Is it right or wrong? God never told them anything about their nakedness being shameful and, therefore, worth covering (2:25). But possessing now, for the first time, their newly acquired prerogative that was God's alone, they decided for themselves that their nakedness was shameful and thus needed covering.

Note, however, God's response to Adam and Eve: "Who told you that you were naked?" (3:11). As far as God was concerned, their nakedness in Eden was not a cause for shame or hiding. Otherwise, he would have told them so. But God would have them trust in his ethical guidance and rest their conscience on his determination regarding what is good and what is evil. So, what was previously part of God's knowledge and prerogative alone is now thrown open to human self-determination. Having tasted independence from God, humanity now has no room to see reality through the lens of their senior partner. From that point on, other issues of good and evil in human existence would be self-determined. Thus, the divine-human partnership in effect was broken, sadly, to the detriment of human well-being.

In addition to this breach in partnership, there is a second reason for the severity and the tragic quality of this incident. By eating from the tree of the knowledge of good and evil, humanity also broke the underlying trust necessary to make the partnership work. Adam and Eve's act showed that they no longer trusted God to have had their best interest at heart when he kept them away from what the tree could offer them. Yet that is so far from the truth when we take the whole of the biblical narrative into account. For God, in fact, wanted humanity ultimately to have the knowledge that the tree offered but in his own good timing.

It is important to note that the tree of the knowledge of good and evil is not, in itself, a bad thing or something that God is permanently keeping away from humanity. John Walton's observation is worth noting here.

> God's prohibition of the tree need not lead us to conclude that there was something wrong with what the tree gave (remember, everything was created "good"). Rather than God's putting the tree there simply to test Adam and Eve, it is more in keeping with his character to understand that the

> tree would have use in the future. When the time was right, the first couple would be able to eat from it.[3]

In other words, Adam and Eve would, indeed, get more or even all of the knowledge of good and evil that they desired, but only in God's proper timing. God knew the proper day and time when humanity would be ready to eat from the tree of the knowledge of good and evil so as to attain as much of the knowledge as God could possibly give. For as we look ahead into what God has in store for humanity, this sort of godlike knowledge is in fact what God promised to give humanity anyway. In 1 John 3:2 we read, "Beloved, now we are children of God, and it has not appeared as yet what we will be. We know that when He appears, we will be like Him, because we will see Him just as He is."

Using a child-rearing analogy, Paul seems to imply in 1 Corinthians 13:11–12 that some knowledge is not yet fitting for us to have because we are still like a child. But one day, when we grow up, God will impart full knowledge to us.

> When I was a child, I used to speak like a child, think like a child, reason like a child; when I became a man, I did away with childish things. For now we see in a mirror dimly, but then face to face; now I know in part, but then I will know fully just as I also have been fully known.

Adam and Eve should have trusted God to be good, loving, and wise. No good thing will he withhold from those who trust him and walk in his ways (Ps. 84:11). Until that day when God fully gives them the godlike knowledge that they desired, however, Adam and Eve need not exist in an impoverished state of ignorance just because they do not have the knowledge of good and evil within themselves. They have their partnership with God to sustain them.

But, as it is, humanity not only breached the formal partnership but also violated the inherent trust necessary for the partnership with God to thrive. Unfortunately, this first failure to trust God, our senior partner, would serve as a tragic paradigm of the human proclivity throughout history, resulting in an inestimable human sense of restlessness and heartaches.

3. Walton, *Genesis*, 205.

Yet, incredibly, the pathway back to human wholeness is as simple as trusting God again. For without this sincere trust in him, whatever obeisance humanity gives to God in its partnership with him would be incomplete in his sight and would ring hollow in the human soul.

From Breaking the Partnership to "Breaking Bad"

Based on this historical and etiological account in Genesis, it is probably safe to say that an important component of how sin is to be understood today is that it is the breach and the continuing breach of the partnership between God and humanity, stemming from the human inclination to not fully trust God, their senior partner. The result has been catastrophic, to say the least, on human existence and flourishing. The following are some ways in which humanity has been adversely affected by the fall into sin.

Alienation from God

After humanity tasted the self-determination of right and wrong, good and evil, which severed the partnership with God, the Bible shows that humans have become a different creature internally. Humankind is no longer willing to assume the role of a junior partner but rather craves the independence of being its own sole determiner of life issues. This then led to a life of habitual sin (independence from God) and, concurrently, to alienation with God.

As God has observed concerning the antediluvian world, so it is in the postdiluvian world we live in: "Then the Lord saw that the wickedness of man was great on the earth, and that every intent of the thoughts of his heart was only evil continually" (Gen. 6:5). Certainly, the apostle Paul would concur when he describes humanity as "all under sin" and says that there is "none righteous, not even one . . . none who seeks for God . . . none who does good" (Rom. 3:9–12). He supports this contention with this vivid description of human fallenness:

> For I know that nothing good dwells in me, that is, in my flesh; for the willing is present in me, but the doing of the good is not. For the good that I want, I do not do, but I practice the very evil that I do not want. But if I am doing the very thing I do not want, I am no longer the one doing it, but sin which dwells in me.

> I find then the principle that evil is present in me, the one who wants to do good. For I joyfully concur with the law of God in the inner man, but I see a different law in the members of my body, waging war against the law of my mind and making me a prisoner of the law of sin which is in my members. Wretched man that I am! Who will set me free from the body of this death? (Rom. 7:18–24)

Martin Luther aptly described fallen humanity as *homo incurvatus in se* ("humanity curved in on itself")—that is, self-centered to the core.[4] To use a modern parlance, Scripture portrays humanity as truly "breaking bad."

With the human condition being what it is, it is not surprising that Isaiah describes the effects of sin as alienating humanity from a holy God:

> But your iniquities have made a separation between you and your God,
> And your sins have hidden His face from you so that He does not hear. (Isa. 59:2)

Such divine alienation manifests itself in the lack of "rest" in human existence. This restlessness in the human soul is first portrayed as physical in quality resulting from the fall. The judgment placed on humanity in Genesis 3 bears this out clearly:

> Then to Adam He said, "Because you have listened to the voice of your wife, and have eaten from the tree about which I commanded you, saying, 'You shall not eat from it';
>
> Cursed is the ground because of you;
> In toil you will eat of it
> All the days of your life.
> Both thorns and thistles it shall grow for you;
> And you will eat the plants of the field;
> By the sweat of your face
> You will eat bread,
> Till you return to the ground,
> Because from it you were taken;

4. Luther, *Lectures on Romans*, 159–60, 182–83, 219–23, 310, 407–8.

For you are dust,
And to dust you shall return." (3:17–19)

Life became difficult after the fall, and humanity has been in a perennial quest for physical rest or security. Thus, when Noah was born, his father Lamech gave him the name "Noah, saying, 'This one will give us rest from our work and from the toil of our hands arising from the ground which the LORD has cursed'" (Gen. 5:29).

But human restlessness, of course, cannot be satisfied on a physical plane alone. So, as the Bible unfolds its grand narrative, it begins to show us that the rest that humanity yearns for is transcendent and spiritual in nature. It can be found only in God. Paul succinctly put it this way in Acts 17:27: "that they [humanity] would seek God, if perhaps they might grope for Him and find Him, though He is not far from each one of us." John Oswalt eloquently explains,

> What is the Biblical understanding of rest? It is the rest of faith, a life of trust, belief, and obedience in God. In him who is eternal there is permanence; in him who has no rival there is security; in him who has made us in his own image there is freedom; in him who combines complete power, complete holiness, and complete love there is tranquility. Those who know these things can silence their fears and anxieties before him (Ps. 131:2), just as he silences the raging seas (65:7 [8]).[5]

Thus, if human existence is to flourish or even survive the weight of sin, this divine alienation must be remedied. Humanity must find its rest in the fullest sense of that word: physical and spiritual rest.

Conflict with Fellow Human Beings

The entrance of sin into human existence affected not only our relationship with God but also our relationship with our fellow human beings. If the nature of sin is the desire for self-determination of right and wrong, good and evil, then it won't be long before we encounter others in the human race who also want to be the final arbiter of such issues for themselves. As one can quickly see, a clash of viewpoints becomes inevitable

5. Oswalt, "Rest," 1135.

and human conflict assured. Human history is full of such disputes stemming from each side wanting to be "the boss." The apostle James asked and answered this perceptive question: "What is the source of quarrels and conflicts among you? Is not the source your pleasures that wage war in your members? You lust and do not have; so you commit murder. You are envious and cannot obtain; so you fight and quarrel" (James 4:1–2). Many of the problems we see in human interrelationships can be traced back to this phenomenon of wanting to be the final arbiter instead of deferring to God and obeying him on such matters.

Exploitation of Creation instead of Creation Care

Aside from its effect on our fellow humans, the fall into sin has also affected the way we treat and care for God's creation in general. Humanity's sense of independence has led us to lean on no one or trust no one but our own selves. Everything in creation has become expedient for the purpose of self-preservation and personal gratification. Our autonomy from God has turned us into usurpers instead of stewards of creation.[6]

For instance, Israel, as a representative of the human race, has shown itself unable to maintain this basic mandate to care for creation. Their stewardship of creation involved the care not just of living creatures but also of the land that they were inhabiting and tilling for their basic agricultural needs. God instructed Israel to give the land a rest every seven years. Leviticus 25:3–5 states,

> Six years you shall sow your field, and six years you shall prune your vineyard and gather in its crop, but during the seventh year the land shall have a sabbath rest, a sabbath to the Lord; you shall not sow your field nor prune your vineyard. Your harvest's aftergrowth you shall not reap, and your grapes of untrimmed vines you shall not gather; the land shall have a sabbatical year.

But Israel failed to do so, no doubt driven by human greed to exploit as much as they could out of a fertile land. Perhaps it was also driven by

6. The care that God expected of humanity is seen in some of his instructions given to Israel. For instance, they were to make sure that their beasts of burden, such as an ox, were properly fed and cared for, especially when these animals were doing their hard work for them (Deut. 25:4). They were to even to give the animals a Sabbath rest just like human beings (Exod. 23:12). Concern for their animals was deemed to be part of Israel's righteousness (Prov. 12:10).

their insecurity regarding the future.[7] Whereas God had the interest of the land at heart, they had their own self-interest in mind. Thus, we read that part of the reason for Israel's exile is seventy years so that the land could enjoy its Sabbath rest for all the years when Israel did not observe this creation care for the land (2 Chron. 36:21).

Interestingly, to the extent that we too are part of creation, humanity's cavalier and self-serving attitude toward creation has also adversely affected us. For in the same way humanity has abused and usurped creation, they have also, strangely enough, done the same to themselves who are also members of the created order. This phenomenon is seen in cases where humankind asserts its freedom to determine matters in life, only to misuse their freedom and become addicted to the wrong choices they have made. While we claim to be free, we are in reality prisoners of our own so-called freedom, reaping and repeatedly receiving the consequences of our decision. Jesus described the human condition this way when speaking to Jews who proudly claimed to be free:

> They answered Him, "We are Abraham's descendants and have never yet been enslaved to anyone; how is it that You say, 'You will become free'?" Jesus answered them, "Truly, truly, I say to you, everyone who commits sin is the slave of sin." (John 8:33–34)

Such is the tragedy of human autonomy. We think that we are free in our self-determination only to discover that we are enslaved to its self-destructive effects.

Aligned with the Enemies of God

Finally, as if the aforementioned consequences were not enough, one other unintended consequence of the fall is that humanity is now aligned

7. On this, God seems to have anticipated their concern and lovingly pointed them to his provision to make possible their obedience on behalf of the land. Leviticus 25:18–22 reads,

> You shall thus observe My statutes and keep My judgments, so as to carry them out, that you may live securely on the land. Then the land will yield its produce, so that you can eat your fill and live securely on it. But if you say, "What are we going to eat on the seventh year if we do not sow or gather in our crops?" then I will so order My blessing for you in the sixth year that it will bring forth the crop for three years. When you are sowing the eighth year, you can still eat old things from the crop, eating the old until the ninth year when its crop comes in.

with the enemies of God. Because we are no longer in right partnership with God, we have become partners with the elements in this world that are opposed to God: the forces of Satan. It is not necessary that we formally swear allegiance to Satan. It is enough that we have de facto sided with him in our own ways. This is clearly one of the Bible's descriptions of fallen humanity in Ephesians 2:1–3:

> And you were dead in your trespasses and sins, in which you formerly walked according to the course of this world, according to the prince of the power of the air, of the spirit that is now working in the sons of disobedience. Among them we too all formerly lived in the lusts of our flesh, indulging the desires of the flesh and of the mind, and were by nature children of wrath, even as the rest.

John 8:44 states this of the devil: he is "a murderer from the beginning, and does not stand in the truth because there is no truth in him. Whenever he speaks a lie, he speaks from his own nature, for he is a liar and the father of lies." So great is Satan's influence based on lies and sinful enticements that the Bible states that "the whole world lies in the power of the evil one" (1 John 5:19). He is the ultimate pusher of human rebellion against the proper partnership with God.

In view of the present human predicament, one might say that humanity has gone from breaking their partnership with God to "breaking bad"—that is, becoming evil not just in their external acts but becoming evil in nature also. As such, death is the right verdict for such a creature who no longer fits the original pattern of God's creation and becomes destructive of God's design. Such a verdict may seem severe but is not at all unusual to our human sensibility.

To illustrate, in the field of forestry, animals in the wild usually are protected and allowed to coexist with human beings because they represent part of nature's ecosystem. However, the moment such a wild animal has its first taste of human blood through violence or has lost the fear of humans, it is generally the policy of the forest rangers to exterminate such a creature.[8] The reason is that such a creature may be the same externally, but

8. Dara Bitler, "Why Do Wildlife Officers Euthanize Bears after They Attack?," *Fox31 News*, May 3, 2021, https://kdvr.com/news/local/why-do-wildlife-officers-euthanize-bears-after-they-attack.

it has changed internally. It no longer contributes to a healthy ecosystem. Its presence works to destroy the equilibrium of the environment. This explains, therefore, why the penalty of sin in the garden of Eden involved not just expulsion from paradise but also death—the elimination of the malignant object from the system (Gen. 2:15–17; Rom. 6:23).

Death comes in at least two different forms for humanity. It happens when physical existence expires. This is the usual concept of death. But death also occurs when we are no longer rightly related to God and, thus, not functioning as we should. One experiences a restlessness within the soul, a kind of ennui of human existence that must be relieved, but, somehow, its resolution cannot be found. It is a form of internal, daily, slow death. An example of this in the Bible is Cain. After murdering Abel his brother, Cain becomes "a vagrant and a wanderer on the earth" (Gen. 4:12). That is, he is one who is far away from the Lord, relationally speaking. Note that his vagrancy and wandering involved his going out "from the presence of the Lord" and settling "in the land of Nod," meaning the land of restless wandering (Gen. 4:16).

While the correct verdict on the human situation is, indeed, death to the human race, which deviated from the original divine purpose, interestingly, this is not exactly what God did to humanity. For he delayed executing the judgment of physical death, as seen in the case of Adam and Eve and their descendants. He also minimized or ameliorated human restlessness resulting from the fall in order to make human existence bearable. But what is most astounding and remarkable about the Bible's portrayal of God is his constant beckoning of humanity to participate once more in their original creation mandate and be his creation-care partners. Those who comply find an ever-increasing measure of the rest that humanity lost after Eden. Such divine beckoning, however, is not without a corresponding divine provision. We now turn to the lifelines that God sent to humanity as part of his seventh-day post-fall providence.

Divine Provision for Patching Up the Broken Partnership in Creation

In one of Jesus's parables, he portrays God acting as a landlord who patiently calls his tenant-partners to give him his share at harvest time (Matt. 21:33–46; Mark 12:1–12; Luke 20:9–16). This remains a fitting picture of God toward humanity in our understanding of his providential dealings with humanity. After the fall, God's relationship with humanity was strained, but God has not rescinded his purposes for humanity to be his creation-care partners. He continues to call them to live out the divine purpose for their existence. Indeed, he holds them accountable to it. To those who do so, he gives meaning and purpose for their existence, which is part of the "rest" that humanity desperately seeks. But those who fail to do so remain in their state of "restlessness."

By doing this, God not only extended to humanity a way of finding personal fulfillment in a fallen world but also utilized human participation to continue governing the world as he designed it—that is, through his chosen agents of humanity. This is not to say that God governs and provides for creation only through willing human participation. God rules creation and often does so even without deliberate human participation or even in the midst of their rebellion against him. His good will for the care of his creation does, indeed, get done on earth as it does in heaven.

But it is important to note that God's modus operandi and preferred method is through his image bearers. This is why he continues to call us to participate despite the fall. This call to participate in the created order is so innate within the human psyche that even a pagan emperor of Rome, Marcus Aurelius, could echo the divine sentiment for humanity:

> Don't you see the plants, the birds, the ants and spiders and bees going about their individual tasks, putting the world in order, as best they can?
> And you're not willing to do your job as a human being?
> Why aren't you running to do what your nature demands?[9]

So how exactly does God gently and creatively draw us back to himself as his creation partners on the seventh day of creation (post-fall)? The following are representative ways in which God provides for humanity to repent and return to their proper partnership relationship with God their senior partner in creation care so as to find rest in their human existence:

- divine forbearance and continuing provision of life
- God's sustaining of the human conscience
- the ordaining of human society and governance

9. Marcus Aurelius, *Meditations* 5.1 (37).

- nature's aesthetics that draw us to return to God
- God's divine involvement and intervention to assist us

Divine Forbearance and Continuing Provision of Life

In their missionary work in Lystra, Paul and Barnabas declare to the inhabitants this gracious yet astonishing statement:

> In the generations gone by He permitted all the nations to go their own ways; and yet He did not leave Himself without witness, in that He did good and gave you rains from heaven and fruitful seasons, satisfying your hearts with food and gladness. (Acts 14:16–17)

Notice God's gracious provision of rain and food for the whole of humanity. Yet the astonishing aspect of this revelation is that God's gracious dealing is conditioned on his having "permitted all the nations to go their own way." In other words, God had to somehow forbear the judgment on the sins of humanity. Indeed, Jesus is even more specific in citing that humanity's moral or ethical condition is not a barrier toward this divine goodness when he instructs his disciples to love their enemies. Jesus puts it this way in Matthew 5:43–45:

> You have heard that it was said, "You shall love your neighbor and hate your enemy." But I say to you, love your enemies and pray for those who persecute you, so that you may be sons of your Father who is in heaven; for He causes His sun to rise on the evil and the good, and sends rain on the righteous and the unrighteous.

This divine forbearance that made possible all kinds of human actions is dramatically demonstrated in the wicked deeds of King Belshazzar, who defiled the temple utensils in Babylon. Daniel rebukes Belshazzar: "You have exalted yourself against the Lord of heaven" by drinking from the sacred utensils while praising "the gods of silver and gold, of bronze, iron, wood and stone, which do not see, hear or understand" (Dan. 5:23). Yet, despite this, God continued to keep Belshazzar alive. As Daniel reminds him, God is the one "in whose hand are your life-breath and all your ways" (5:23). In short, God was keeping Belshazzar alive even as the king was blaspheming him. That God should allow sinful human beings to continue to breathe

the air he gives even as they mock and sin against him is truly amazing and the hallmark of divine goodness toward fallen humanity.

The goal of this act of divine forbearance, however, is not mere toleration of sin but the granting of opportunity for human rehabilitation to occur, as indicated in Acts 17:30:

> Therefore having overlooked the times of ignorance, God is now declaring to men that all people everywhere should repent, because He has fixed a day in which He will judge the world in righteousness.

For, indeed, as the psalmist says in Psalm 130:3–4, God's kindness is intended to lead us to a proper relationship with him:

> If You, Lord, should mark iniquities,
> O Lord, who could stand?
> But there is forgiveness with You,
> That You may be feared.

Like Belshazzar, King Nebuchadnezzar also acted foolishly against God by proudly thinking of his kingdom as his own personal accomplishment instead of giving God the proper credit. In response, God consigned him to live like an animal for a season. Some speculate the condition to be a kind of psychological malady. But no one knows for certain except that it was a divine judgment.

Though Nebuchadnezzar experienced divine judgment, amazingly God did not exterminate his life but rather sustained it. This gave Nebuchadnezzar time to properly respond to God's providential kindness as he later came to the correct realization. He then unequivocally declared,

> But at the end of that period, I, Nebuchadnezzar, raised my eyes toward heaven and my reason returned to me, and I blessed the Most High and praised and honored Him who lives forever;
>
> For His dominion is an everlasting dominion,
> And His kingdom endures from generation to generation.
> All the inhabitants of the earth are accounted as nothing,
> But He does according to His will in the host of heaven
> And among the inhabitants of earth;

> And no one can ward off His hand
> Or say to Him, "What have You done?" (Dan. 4:34–35)

Behind every Nebuchadnezzar-type act of repentance in human history lies God's divine forbearance to keep such a person alive so that such an act of repentance and, eventually, a return to partnership with God in creation care could happen again.

God's Sustaining of the Human Conscience

For humanity to return to a proper partnership with God, he must sustain our "life breath" so that we have the opportunity to repent and return. But repentance requires more than physical life breath; it also requires a functioning conscience to be able to respond to right or wrong. The human conscience is part of what God has imparted when he created humankind in his image. Bound up in the *imago Dei* is a functioning human conscience. Despite humanity's fall into sin, the image of God in humankind has not been eradicated. Humanity has not become another type of species or a lower creature. The *imago Dei*, which contains the conscience, remains intact, albeit marred or distorted—not in full capacity, so to speak.

In most instances, humanity can discern the proper course of action that approximates God's general purposes for creation. That is due to God's gift of conscience through the *imago Dei*. The apostle Paul says this in Romans 2:14–15:

> For when Gentiles who do not have the Law do instinctively the things of the Law, these, not having the Law, are a law to themselves, in that they show the work of the Law written in their hearts, their conscience bearing witness and their thoughts alternately accusing or else defending them.

Thus, theologians recognize that even the most irreligious persons know instinctively through their conscience what is the ethical thing to do in a given situation. Granted, of course, they may not necessarily act on their conscience or, worse, even suppress the faint voice of conscience within them.

Mario Puzo's novel *The Godfather* tells the story of the rise of the Corleone crime family in New York. In one incident, an old lady who was about to be evicted from her apartment because she had a noisy dog decided to ask Vito Corleone for help to speak to her landlord that she might keep her pet. The crime boss had nothing to gain in this messy landlord-tenant squabble, which might even be considered beneath him. Yet, out of compassion for the old lady, he did. When the landlord found out who was intervening on the lady's behalf, he rescinded her eviction notice, allowed her to keep the dog, and even lowered the lady's rent.[10]

While this story is humorous and heartwarming, no one reading this account would find it implausible for a mafia don to feel for the lady and act on her behalf. For it is observable in many walks of life that the human conscience is capable of directing fallen individuals to do things that are not purely out of self-interest alone but altruistic. So whenever we allow the human conscience to function properly, we are, more often than not, on our way back to becoming partners with God again, at least in a given situation.

The Ordaining of Human Society and Governance

A well-functioning good conscience holds promise that humanity could still return to its partnership with God. But the grip of sin in the human soul must never be underestimated. Sin makes the human conscience not always dependable. For instance, humanity can reject the inner work of conscience to guide them and, thus, suffer "shipwreck in regard to their faith" (1 Tim. 1:19). Moreover, sin could also sear the human conscience to render it ineffective and insensitive. Paul states in 1 Timothy 4:1–2,

> But the Spirit explicitly says that in later times some will fall away from the faith, paying attention to deceitful spirits and doctrines of demons, by means of the hypocrisy of liars seared in their own conscience as with a branding iron.

In such a situation, something stronger is necessary to guide the conscience to do what is right so as turn the human heart back to partnership with God in creation care.

One such way is through the divine provision of government. By government, I mean not simply political governance but any kind of human

10. William Fisher, "'The Godfather': Key Changes to Vito Corleone from Book to Screen," *Collider*, March 19, 2022, https://collider.com/the-godfather-vito-corleone-book-movie-differences-explained.

governance that promotes proper order and structure in human society so that humanity functions as God intended them to as partners with God in the care of his creation. Certainly, these governing structures in human society may not always be aware that they are engaged in such partnership with God and his purposes.

The Bible not only supports the presence of such institutions in human existence but also explicitly states that they are ordained by God for the good of all. Paul states in Romans 13:1, "Every person is to be in subjection to the governing authorities. For there is no authority except from God, and those which exist are established by God." Concurring, Peter states the same in 1 Peter 2:13–14: "Submit yourselves for the Lord's sake to every human institution, whether to a king as the one in authority, or to governors." And the divine purpose for such institutions is that they are established by God "for the punishment of evildoers and the praise of those who do right" (1 Pet. 2:14). Paul repeats the same sentiment as Peter but emphasizes the intended divine effect of government on the human conscience: "Therefore it is necessary to be in subjection [to government], not only because of wrath [i.e., punishment], but also for conscience' sake" (Rom. 13:5).

As stated previously, "governing authorities" and "human institution" could also include wider societal structures such as the familial and household relationships. Thus, the Bible emphasizes the importance of such relationships as part of what brings stability to life. In living within the societal expectation of one's station in life, one can glorify God by growing in good personal conscience and by contributing to the common good of society. There are many explicit teachings in the New Testament of such societal codes of ethics, which Martin Luther referred to as *Haustafeln*, found in passages such as Ephesians 5:15–33; 6:1–9; Colossians 3:18–25; 4:1; 1 Peter 2:13–25; 3:1–22.

When these societal structures are functioning properly, Paul seems to imply, it leads to "a tranquil and quiet life in all godliness and dignity. This is good and acceptable in the sight of God our Savior, who desires all men to be saved and to come to the knowledge of the truth" (1 Tim. 2:2–4).

In modern parlance, it leads to peace and order in society. Following these orderly ways of conducting oneself or one's business in society could translate into a smooth delivery of goods and services worldwide for the betterment of humanity such as an efficient flow of the supply chain. But failure to abide by these God-ordained structures could lead to societal disaster. It does not take much imagination to see what would happen to God's good creation should individuals choose to violate their conscience or act in a manner that spurns the common good. Human governance as ordained by God, therefore, has a way of restraining evils in the world and even influences an individual's personal development, putting humanity back in a position to be God's creation partner again.[11]

Nature's Aesthetics That Draw Us to Return to God

What also contributes to the sustaining of the human conscience is the simple beauty or aesthetics in the created order. Theologians call this general revelation. In this way, God provides something subtle to draw humanity back to the awareness of him. It is a gentle reminder of our earthiness and our role in creation. This gaze at the aesthetics of creation eventually leads our gaze back to a creator to whom we are accountable (Heb. 4:13). As Paul says in Romans 1:20, "For since the creation of the world His invisible attributes, His eternal power and divine nature, have been clearly seen, being understood through what has been made, so that they are without excuse." Additionally, the psalmist puts it this way:

> The heavens are telling of the glory of God;
> And their expanse is declaring the work of His hands.
> Day to day pours forth speech,
> And night to night reveals knowledge.
> There is no speech, nor are there words;
> Their voice is not heard.
> Their line has gone out through all the earth. (Ps. 19:1–4)

Indeed, to the extent that humanity is part of creation, there is something about us that also emanates God and reminds us of him. Paul could make this bold statement: "That which is known about God is evident within them; for God made it evident to them" (Rom. 1:19).

11. Naturally, this observance of the *Haustafeln* principle is to be done in a biblically discerning way, always being aware that the ideal can be co-opted by evil. Thus, necessary adjustments, at times, must be done in order to do justice to the *Haustafeln* principle. Peter's words in Acts 5:29 serves as a guide: "We must obey God rather than men."

There is something in the human soul that cries out to care for the great expanse of the created order. We do so not merely for our own self-preservation but for the sheer beauty of it. This could happen in the form of a grand-scale work of conserving earth's resources or in the form of creating simple art from the stuff of earth. As Daniel Pink observes of humanity, "The most deeply motivated people—not to mention those who are most productive and satisfied—hitch their desires to a cause larger than themselves. . . . From the moment that human beings first stared into the sky, contemplated their place in the universe, and tried to create something that bettered the world and outlasted their lives, we have been purpose seekers."[12] Through these ways, humanity is indirectly reminded of and driven back to the God who called them to be his creation partners. In fact, nature's aesthetics are both vocationally clarifying and therapeutically satisfying to the soul. There is something restorative and direction-setting in the messages that nature emanates.

God's Divine Involvement and Intervention to Assist Us

Thus far, the kinds of provision we have seen are those that God had laid out at the time of creation. In other words, they are part of the preexisting structure or fabric of the created order that God, in turn, uses to bring humanity back to himself in partnership. But God's gracious provision as evinced in the seventh day of creation also includes an extemporaneous kind of provision. That is, God reacts and responds to the human predicament outside the norm or routine of the created order. Here, God intervenes in human affairs in a more direct fashion, usually in unexpected or even supernatural ways depending on the situation at hand.

Under this category of providence, we see its most basic example in the form of human supplication to God and his responding to our prayer in direct and yet creative ways. In time of need, God makes himself accessible to us. Such a characteristic makes us turn to him in both supplication and repentance. Psalm 145:17–19 puts it this way:

> The Lord is righteous in all His ways
> And kind in all His deeds.
> The Lord is near to all who call upon Him,
> To all who call upon Him in truth.

12. Pink, *Drive*, 131–32.

> He will fulfill the desire of those who fear Him;
> He will also hear their cry and will save them.

God's extemporaneous providence, though, goes beyond what we ourselves can ask of him. There are times when he will unilaterally act on our behalf because the situation calls for it and we do not always know what to pray for (Rom. 8:26). One such instance is in the restraining of evil in the unseen realm that has an adverse effect on humanity. The apostle Paul describes how there is a "mystery of lawlessness" at work in the world today (2 Thess. 2:5–7). But there is a restraining force that is countervailing the power of lawlessness, indeed, restraining it from creating more havoc in human existence. Many theologians believe, rightly, that this restraining force is none other than God himself working to ameliorate the effects of evil in the world.

In this extemporaneous way of providing for the needs of fallen humanity, God shows himself to be a reliable and desirable partner through the vicissitudes of human existence. His providence is not automated but responsive and tailor-made to our individual needs. And as humanity returns to their role once again as God's agents of ruling and caring for his creation, his providence serves to give humanity the rest that their restless souls desperately seek.

Common Grace and Providence

The goal of this chapter is not to provide a comprehensive list of how God provides but rather to give a sense to the reader of God's seventh-day post-fall providence. From the discussion above, one may get the impression that providence includes what theologians call "common grace."[13] This certainly is the case. Though God's providence is more than just common grace,[14] common grace is an integral part of God's providence that deserves to be dwelled upon and celebrated. Too often, reference to common grace as a subset of providence gets short shrift in theological works.

13. John Murray defines common grace as "every favour of whatever kind or degree, falling short of salvation, which this undeserving and sin-cursed world enjoys at the hand of God." Murray, "Common Grace," 96. Similarly, Wayne Grudem defines it as "the grace of God by which he gives people innumerable blessings that are not part of salvation." Grudem, *Systematic Theology*, 1238.

14. See Helm, *Providence of God*, 119.

This chapter has given proper importance to God's common grace in his providential work after the fall. If there is any good thing that happens in the world through humanity, it is never apart from God's common grace. The movie *Schindler's List* depicts the real-life heroic story of Oskar Schindler, who singlehandedly saved 1,200 Jews from death camps during World War II. He did it by taking big risks of continuously using his connection to the German military as a businessman. Near the end of the movie, when Schindler had to separate from the Jews he saved, they paid him tribute with a Hebrew saying from the Talmud: "Whoever saves one life, saves the world entire." It was a touching scene as it reminded Schindler that what he did, with mixed motives at times, turned out to be his greatest contribution to humanity. Because of what he did, countless generations of people would live and carry on the human race. And, indeed, as the movie ends, the generations that sprang from the lives he saved were movingly put on display on the movie screen.[15]

While the movie may not attribute Schindler's ability to save these Jews to God, could anyone deny the role that God's providence played in his good deeds? As we noted earlier in this chapter, there is a work in the world today of

- divine forbearance and continuing provision of life
- God's sustaining of the human conscience
- the ordaining of human society and governance
- nature's aesthetics that draw us to return to God
- God's divine involvement and intervention to assist us

Schindler's life proves what Ecclesiastes 3:12–13 says about the ideal life: "I know that there is nothing better for them [humanity] than to rejoice and to do good in one's lifetime; moreover, that every man who eats and drinks sees good in all his labor—it is the gift of God." It is, indeed, God's gift of grace to Schindler or anybody else, for that matter, who is able to accomplish anything worthwhile in this life. What this chapter is arguing, therefore, is that humanity's great and noble acts are not theirs alone. They are part of God's gracious and continuing seventh-day creation providence post-fall.

15. "Schindler's List—'I Didn't Do Enough,'" YouTube video, 1:36, posted by Universal Pictures, December 3, 2019, https://youtu.be/W9vj2Wf57rQ.

To that end, two beneficial side effects befell Schindler. First, whether he was aware of it or not, Schindler became God's partner in creation care, to be specific, in the saving of lives. Second, he was able to find a measure of rest for his soul. After the war, Schindler's life did not necessarily go smoothly. His marriage ended in divorce. His business ventures did not again flourish as they did during the war. In other words, his life was filled with restless concerns. But in the midst of all of that, one thing that constantly gave him rest and security was the Jews he was able to rescue. Somehow, they became to him a tangible as well as moral source of comfort in life. Those like Schindler who would appropriate God's seventh-day creation providence (however imperfectly) likewise can expect to find a measure of rest for their restless souls as they reenter into partnership with God in creation's care.

The Beckoning Call of a Partner Unheeded

When Jim Monaghan left Domino's Pizza, the door back to his partnership with his brother Tom Monaghan became forever closed to him. But God's partnership with humanity is not like that. When humanity left their partnership with God, he continued to beckon them to return and, indeed, provided the means by which they could act as his partners in creation care again. Such means come in the form of common grace. When acted upon, common grace as part of God's providence can bring about a measure of rest to the human soul amid a world fallen into sin. And, in the process, God fulfills his desired modus operandi of ruling creation through humanity, his image bearers.

There is, however, a tragic quality to this biblical account. Despite God's gracious extension of his providential assistance, humanity is dead set on going "solo" while they live in God's good creation. One might say that eating from the tree of the knowledge of good and evil has had an enduring effect on humanity. Unfortunately, this failure to remain in partnership with God perpetuates an endless cycle of human restlessness.

A passage in Isaiah 30 captures well the tragic nature of the human predicament. Although originally spoken to Judah, this passage surely also describes the condition of the entire human race:

> For thus the Lord GOD, the Holy One of Israel, has said,
> "In repentance and rest you will be saved,
> In quietness and trust is your strength."
> But you were not willing,
> And you said, "No, for we will flee on horses,"
> Therefore you shall flee!
> "And we will ride on swift horses,"
> Therefore those who pursue you shall be swift.
> One thousand will flee at the threat of one man;
> You will flee at the threat of five,
> Until you are left as a flag on a mountain top
> And as a signal on a hill.
> Therefore the LORD longs to be gracious to you,
> And therefore He waits on high to have compassion on you.
> For the LORD is a God of justice;
> How blessed are all those who long for Him. (Isa. 30:15–18)

In view of this human resistance against finding rest in God, will God do more to draw humanity back to partnership with him? Amazingly, he does. And it now involves what I have termed the eighth day of creation providence.

5

God's Providence in the "Not Yet" of the Eighth Day of Creation

Turning and turning in the widening gyre
The falcon cannot hear the falconer;
Things fall apart; the centre cannot hold;
Mere anarchy is loosed upon the world,
The blood-dimmed tide is loosed, and everywhere
The ceremony of innocence is drowned;
The best lack all conviction, while the worst
Are full of passionate intensity.
Surely some revelation is at hand;
Surely the Second Coming is at hand.

—W. B. Yeats, "The Second Coming"

Behold, as the eyes of servants look to the hand of their
master,
As the eyes of a maid to the hand of her mistress,
So our eyes look to the LORD our God,
Until He is gracious to us.

—Psalm 123:2

The Helpless Human Yearning for More to Life

On June 18, 1815, two of the greatest military commanders of all time engaged in an epic battle at Waterloo. On one side was Napoleon Bonaparte, leading the French army. And on the other side was the Duke of Wellington, leading a coalition army. Both leaders did their best to achieve the goal of victory against each other. But the battle hung on the balance of reinforcement. Napoleon counted on the arrival of Marshal Grouchy and the Duke of Wellington on Marshal Blücher.

One might say that, while actively fighting, both Napoleon and Wellington were also engaged in active waiting for the reinforcements needed to win. Both commanders must have felt helpless knowing that nothing of their effort or ingenuity would change the tide of the battle until aid from outside arrived. Literally, victory was outside their control. It depended on the good judgment and the reliability of the respective marshals they counted on for reinforcement.

Alas, only Marshal Blücher arrived at the Battle of Waterloo, marking Wellington's eventual victory and sealing Napoleon's defeat. To this day no one knows for sure why Marshal Grouchy did not come through for Napoleon. But no one disputes that the outcome at Waterloo might have been different had he done so. And no one disputes that Napoleon did everything within his power to win. But, to really win, Napoleon had to wait for outside assistance that unfortunately never arrived.[1]

This vignette from military history in many ways pictures the human condition. Like Napoleon and Wellington at the Battle of Waterloo, humanity must actively "fight" to survive and to find a measure of "rest" in life. Such is human existence on the seventh day of creation. But the ultimate "rest" that humanity longs for cannot be found through human effort alone, for there are matters beyond human ability to resolve. These issues touch on human mortality and eternal destiny. Until these matters are resolved, humanity cannot achieve true rest. Theologian Carl Braaten makes the following poignant observation about the human race:

1. Shannon Selin, "Napoleon on Waterloo—What Did Bonaparte Actually Say about His Most Famous Defeat?," *Military History Now*, November 19, 2019, https://militaryhistorynow.com/2019/11/19/napoleon-on-waterloo-what-did-historys-greatest-conqueror-say-about-his-most-famous-defeat.

> Man as man is afflicted by a hunger for love, healing, freedom, and righteousness that cannot be satisfied by any of the structures with which he is allied in the present time. Man has a passion to be wholly human that cannot be satisfied by the roles he plays and the houses and cars he owns or by the success he gains in his upward strivings. When he races into the future or turns the clock ahead, he is only shortening the distance between now and his time for dying.[2]

It is absolutely at this juncture that humanity is in a predicament similar to that of Napoleon and Wellington. God has to provide "reinforcement" if life truly is to be complete. As humbling as it is, humanity's role on these grand matters of life is to simply wait—that is, hope in God. Reinhold Niebuhr wisely states, "It is not within man's power to solve the vexing problem of his subjection to, and partial independence from, the flex of time," and, indeed, goes on to say that "evil is introduced into history by the very effort of men to solve this problem by their own resources."[3] Thus, in the end, humanity is forced to agree and pine with William Yeats, "Surely some revelation is at hand; / Surely the Second Coming is at hand."

Christian Hope and Worldly Hope: Both Legitimate Passive Expectation

Wellington's victory in Waterloo provides a picture of "reinforcement" from outside needed to address issues beyond our ability to control. While this concept of deliverance is Christian in nature, it is not unique to Christianity. The idea of and, indeed, the desire for deliverance are universal. Thus, the Christian's hope of a future deliverance (eschatology) is not a fantastic or unusual hope that no one else could relate to. In fact, it is seen even in secular worldviews, albeit without the mention of God.

The philosopher Karl Löwith made the observation that today's Western secular philosophy (founded in Hegel, Comte, Voltaire, Marx, Heidegger, and their progenies) possesses an optimistic view of the future. But instead of God as the basis of its confidence for deliverance, it is based on the march of human progress. Löwith says, "The belief in an immanent and indefinite progress replaces more and more the belief in God's

2. Braaten, *Christ and the Counter-Christ*, 50–51.
3. Niebuhr, *Nature and Destiny of Man*, 287.

transcendent providence."[4] Thus, this optimistic philosophical outlook has become a religion of progress. Interestingly, he notes further that the "structure" of Western secularism's "leading idea of progress" is "Christian by derivation" but is also "anti-Christian by implication" because it has appropriated the Christian notion of providence to the explicit exclusion of the God of the Bible.[5] Concurring, Reinhold Niebuhr says,

> The whole of modern utopianism is thus implicit in Renaissance spirituality. The "idea of progress," the most characteristic and firmly held article in the *credo* of modern man, is the inevitable philosophy of history emerging from the Renaissance. This result was achieved by combining the classical confidence in man with the Biblical confidence in the meaningfulness of history. It must be observed, however, that history is given a simpler meaning than that envisaged in the prophetic-Biblical view.[6]

The optimistic "progress of human history" is denuded of God, and God's providence has become a mere impersonal force at work. Philosopher Charles Taylor has dubbed this phenomenon "providential deism."[7]

Be that as it may, what this means is that both Christian eschatological hope and Western secular eschatological hope are not far apart in their understanding of how to relate to the future. Both would acknowledge that there is nothing one can do about the future but hope for the best outcome. There is a passive quality to this future hope that both worldviews acknowledge. In short, both require a faith that hopes. Indeed, as Emil Brunner describes of the Christian understanding, "Faith is the capitulation of man before God, the utter despair of what one is and does, it requires wholly the attitude of passivity and receptivity. In the act of believing you *do* nothing, you merely *get* something. . . . Faith is first quiet, peace, rest; the turmoil of the soul is silenced; the strain of striving has come to an end, for as a believer one *has* and *is*."[8]

Despite the similarity in eschatological hope, there are differences that must be stressed between these two hopes for the future. There are two major areas in which the differences can be seen: first, the specificity of the

4. Löwith, *Meaning in History*, 60.
5. Löwith, *Meaning in History*, 61.
6. Niebuhr, *Nature and Destiny of Man*, 154–55.
7. Taylor, *A Secular Age*, 221–321.
8. Brunner, *Theology of Crisis*, 83–84.

Christian hope of God's providence for the future; second, the means for obtaining God's future providential blessing as grounded in the person of Jesus Christ. By attending to these two main differences, we see that not only is the Christian hope differentiated from the secular hope that is prevalent in Western culture today but also, more importantly, the inquirer (regardless of which culture he or she may be from) is allowed to answer to one's own satisfaction Immanuel Kant's deeply existential question: "What may I hope?"[9]

The Promise of an Eighth Day of Creation

In the Bible's metanarrative, God promises to bring about a new creation. If he rested on the seventh day of creation, he will once again create. Thus, he will usher in an eighth day of creation, so to speak. In that day, all the human yearning for more to life will be fulfilled. In this chapter, we will see from Scripture how the world will be re-created on the eighth day for the benefit of fallen humanity as well as the created order. Scripture, as far back as the Old Testament, has always anticipated an eschaton whereby God would deliver humanity from its fallen state. Walther Eichrodt says that there is a "remarkable agreement [among Scripture writers] . . . in a return of Paradise as the ultimate goal of God's Providence, and in the appearance of a superhuman ruler-figure [as God's agent to bring that about]."[10] Hebrews 4:3–11 states,

> For we who have believed enter that rest, just as He has said,
>
> > "As I swore in My wrath,
> > They shall not enter My rest,"
>
> although His works were finished from the foundation of the world. For He has said somewhere concerning the seventh day: "And God rested on the seventh day from all His works"; and again in this passage, "They shall not enter My rest." Therefore, since it remains for some to enter it, and those who formerly had good news preached to them failed to enter because of disobedience, He again fixes a certain day, "Today," saying through David after so long a time just as has been said before,
>
> > "Today if you hear His voice,
> > Do not harden your hearts."

9. Kant, *Critique of Pure Reason*, 677.
10. Eichrodt, *Theology of the Old Testament*, 1:473.

> For if Joshua had given them rest, He would not have spoken of another day after that. So there remains a Sabbath rest for the people of God. For the one who has entered His rest has himself also rested from his works, as God did from His. Therefore let us be diligent to enter that rest, so that no one will fall, through following the same example of disobedience.

As we look at the greater rest that God has in store for humanity on the eighth day of creation, our discussion would seem like a foray into eschatology, soteriology, and Christology. In a sense, it is. For it is inevitable that these subdisciplines in Christian theology should come into play. One cannot adequately consider the panoply of God's providential expressions for the benefit of humanity without also considering these theological areas.[11] We do so, however, judiciously and limiting their inclusion insofar as they relate directly to the doctrine of providence.

Generally speaking, the Bible takes as axiomatic that when humanity fulfills its role as God's junior partner, humanity can receive God's benediction of "rest" from the toils of life. But even for those who experience this blessing of "rest," there remains in them a restlessness of the soul. We see this human restlessness in at least four areas: (1) human mortality (death), (2) injustice in the world (evil), (3) lack of intimacy with God (meaninglessness), and (4) pain and suffering in life (hardships). In this chapter we explore why this is so, and we examine the means by which God's providence addresses these areas that are future-oriented in nature.

1. Human Mortality (Death): The Resurrection of the Body

Before he died, Steve Jobs, the legendary founder of Apple, expressed his wistful desire for an afterlife to his biographer Walter Isaacson this way: "I like to think that something survives after you die. It's strange to think that you accumulate all this experience, and maybe a little wisdom, and it just goes away. So I really want to believe that something survives,

11. John Webster describes the theology of providence "as informed by other tracts of Christian teaching—most of all the doctrine of God, but also, for example, creation, soteriology and anthropology. Attending to these connections helps to preserve Christian specificity; their neglect can issue in one of the most common disorders in an account of providence, namely dominance of questions or modes of argument not derived from Christian confession." Webster, *God without Measure*, 129.

that maybe your consciousness endures." But, after a long pause, he attempts to correct himself by saying, "But on the other hand, perhaps it's like an on-off switch. *Click!* And you're gone." Then, just when we think he has expressed his denial of an afterlife, he reveals his true sentiment with this concrete expression of belief. With a smile, Steve Jobs says, "Maybe that's why I never liked to put on-off switches on Apple devices."[12]

So, for those of us who own Apple products, we have a perennial reminder in our electronic devices of Steve Jobs's yearning for a continuation of life after death. Such a sentiment, though, is found not only among billionaires and captains in industry but also in every human soul in the world. Whether one explicitly states it or not, life is precious. Everyone wants to prolong their existence in the world. And we organize our life in response to this impending mortal destiny.

There is a practice today among those who look to science for a solution to the problem of human mortality. It is called cryogenics, whereby one's body is frozen immediately after death in the hope that science will one day be able to bring the dead back to life. The fact that there are those who want to do this despite science's inability to raise the dead shows how precious life is and how desperate humanity is to extend life. After the issues of our daily toils are taken care of, prolonging life is the next big issue that eludes humanity. Until this matter is resolved, there is no ultimate rest for the human soul.

The Bible recognizes that death is an enemy to humankind—one that has filled humanity with great fear. But does God have a provision for this deepest of human problems? Indeed, God intends for this enemy to be defeated one day. Paul says, "The last enemy that will be abolished is death" (1 Cor. 15:26). The way God will defeat death is not merely with the continuation of human existence in spirit form after death, but the impartation of a new resurrected body like Christ's to go along with a regenerated soul. God will resurrect those who are dead and give them a resurrected body that is so superior in quality that death no longer has a hold on it. As Paul says, "But when this perishable [mortal body] will have put on the imperishable [resurrected body], and this mortal will have put on immortality, then will come about the saying that is written, 'Death is

12. Isaacson, *Steve Jobs*, 740.

swallowed up in victory. O death, where is your victory? O death, where is your sting?'" (1 Cor. 15:54–55). Ultimately, this is what Steve Jobs was secretly desiring and hoping for.

Without this resurrection hope, humanity is enslaved by the fear of death and its many side effects. One such residual effect is human despair that cannot be placated with worldly success. It causes a person ultimately to conclude, "If the dead are not raised, let us eat and drink, for tomorrow we die" (1 Cor. 15:32). But the opposite is true. Possessing a hope of the resurrection of the body, one is emboldened to live life with gusto.

Indeed, one of the earliest references to the resurrection of the body in the Hebrew mindset can be found in the book of 2 Maccabees. There, King Antiochus arrested seven brothers for observing the Mosaic dietary laws despite his prohibition of such observance. These brothers bravely faced a cruel death rather than forsake God's laws. The reason they were able to remain true to their religious conviction despite torture and violent death was their belief in a future resurrection of their body. As the account shows, as one of the brothers was about to be tortured, "he quickly put out his tongue and courageously stretched forth his hands, and said nobly, 'I got these from Heaven, and because of his [God's] laws I disdain them, and from him I hope to get them back again'" (2 Macc. 7:10–11 RSV).

In the New Testament, we also see the same boldness that comes from the promise of a resurrected body. Many early believers were emboldened to suffer and even die for Christ's sake. First John 3:2–3 states it this way: "Beloved, now we are children of God, and it has not appeared as yet what we will be. We know that when He appears, we will be like Him, because we will see Him just as He is. And everyone who has this hope fixed on Him purifies himself, just as He is pure." Even more graphically, the apostle John says in the book of Revelation,

> Then I saw thrones, and they sat on them, and judgment was given to them. And I saw the souls of those who had been beheaded because of their testimony of Jesus and because of the word of God, and those who had not worshiped the beast or his image, and had not received the mark on their forehead and on their hand; and they came to life and reigned with Christ for a thousand years. . . . This is the first resurrection. (Rev. 20:4–5)

The Christian view of resurrection as part of the afterlife is one of the clearest ways in which God has providentially acted to satisfy the human longing for a continued embodied existence. Indeed, when seen properly, God promises not just to reembody humanity but to do so in a way that is better than its original state. It will be a reembodiment in the same manner as Jesus's resurrected body. But, alas, the appreciation of this teaching needs to be revived within many Christian communities because we seem to have become satisfied with a spiritualized existence without a reembodied existence, thus nullifying this important providential act of God.[13]

2. Injustice in the World (Evil): A New Heaven and a New Earth

Evil abounds in the world today. Regardless of one's religious orientation or lack thereof, the human soul desires an existence that is free of evil. It may be utopian in aspiration, but humankind cannot live without this desire. John Lennon's anthem "Imagine" captures well this sentiment. Despite its seeming naivete, the song's enduring popularity is indicative of the deep human desire for a world such as Lennon is describing, one where "all the people" are "living life in peace."

How does God respond to this human yearning for a world without evil or injustice? Interestingly, far from discouraging such a desire, he stokes and intensifies it by promising to make it come true. The world as we know it will be transformed. There will be a re-formation of heaven and earth that marks the eighth day of creation. Both Isaiah and the apostle John describe it as the creation of a new heaven and a new earth (Isa. 65:17; Rev. 21:1). Its newness can be seen in the effects on earth's inhabitants. Isaiah 11:6–9 gives this astonishing description of a new world unlike the present one:

> And the wolf will dwell with the lamb,
> And the leopard will lie down with the young goat,
> And the calf and the young lion and the fatling together;
> And a little boy will lead them.
> Also the cow and the bear will graze,
> Their young will lie down together,

13. See, e.g., the critiques offered by Wright, *Surprised by Hope*; Middleton, *A New Heaven*.

> And the lion will eat straw like the ox.
> The nursing child will play by the hole of the cobra,
> And the weaned child will put his hand on the viper's den.
> They will not hurt or destroy in all My holy mountain,
> For the earth will be full of the knowledge of the LORD
> As the waters cover the sea.

Wild animals and humans usually end up harming one another. Living in peace and harmony with one another is not the norm. But in that future existence, it is.

In addition, Revelation 21:1 gives an enigmatic description of that coming new heaven and new earth. It says that "the first heaven and the first earth passed away, and there is no longer any sea." Why is there no sea in that future world? What could that possibly mean? The sea is a representation of evil in the book of Revelation. It is the portal from which evil beings in Revelation come out to wreak havoc in the world. By stating that there will be no more sea, the apostle John's vision is pointing us to a world without evil in it. The portal will be closed and completely eradicated. In short, it will be a time just as God himself said, "Behold, I am making all things new" (Rev. 21:5). It is a new day in creation, an eighth day.

Judgment of Sinners (Punishment)

Life is not always fair. The wicked seem to get away with their sins and even prosper in the midst of their moral compromise. For the righteous who strive to do God's will, it is very discouraging. It can even be a stumbling block. The book of Psalms muses upon this theme a lot but also provides the divine response to it. Perhaps this is one reason why this ancient poetic book of the Bible is so relevant in speaking to and soothing the human sense of justice even today.

For instance, the psalmist Asaph expresses life's unfairness bluntly this way:

> Behold, these are the wicked;
> And always at ease, they have increased in wealth.
> Surely in vain I have kept my heart pure
> And washed my hands in innocence;

> For I have been stricken all day long
> And chastened every morning. (Ps. 73:12–14)

But what changes such a view for the righteous and causes them to persevere is the reality of a day of judgment of sinners where the wrong will ultimately be made right. Asaph puts it this way:

> When I pondered to understand this,
> It was troublesome in my sight
> Until I came into the sanctuary of God;
> Then I perceived their end.
> Surely You set them in slippery places;
> You cast them down to destruction.
> How they are destroyed in a moment!
> They are utterly swept away by sudden terrors!
> Like a dream when one awakes,
> O Lord, when aroused, You will despise their form. (Ps. 73:16–20)

Such a day of judgment is envisioned precisely as part of God's providence known as the eighth day of creation. The righteous will be vindicated and the wicked will receive what is due them. For no one escapes the justice of God. Throughout the Old Testament this future day of judgment is described as the day of the Lord.[14]

The New Testament is even more graphic in its description of this final day of judgment. The apostle John shares his inspired vision of the final judgment:

> Then I saw a great white throne and Him who sat upon it, from whose presence earth and heaven fled away, and no place was found for them. And I saw the dead, the great and the small, standing before the throne, and books were opened; and another book was opened, which is the book of life; and the dead were judged from the things which were written in the books, according to their deeds. And the sea gave up the dead which were in it, and death and Hades gave up the dead which were in them; and they were judged, every one of them according to their deeds. (Rev. 20:11–13)

14. See House, "Day of the Lord."

Note specifically how judgment will be executed on that day:

> And He who sits on the throne said, "Behold, I am making all things new." And He said, "Write, for these words are faithful and true." Then He said to me, "It is done. I am the Alpha and the Omega, the beginning and the end. I will give to the one who thirsts from the spring of the water of life without cost. He who overcomes will inherit these things, and I will be his God and he will be My son. But for the cowardly and unbelieving and abominable and murderers and immoral persons and sorcerers and idolaters and all liars, their part will be in the lake that burns with fire and brimstone, which is the second death." (Rev. 21:5–8)

Thus, Asaph's search for a day of ultimate judgment of the wicked is fulfilled on the eighth day of creation. God has provided a day of ultimate justice to satisfy the human soul.

Interestingly, Psalm 92 carries with it the title "A Song for the Sabbath Day." If the superscription is, indeed, true, then one could easily presume that the meditation contained therein is what the ancient Israelites used for Sabbath day observance. The psalm begins with a call to praise God for his works (vv. 1–5). Then it unashamedly and unapologetically acknowledges the reality that, in this present world, the wicked do sprout up like grass. Those who do iniquity do flourish (vv. 6–7a). But they do so only "that they might be destroyed forevermore" (v. 7b). In short, there will be a day of reckoning, for the Lord is on high and his enemies will be rightly judged one day (vv. 8–9). As for the righteous, they can rest secure that their cause does not escape God's notice. The psalm provides a contrast to the fleeting prosperity of the wicked, who are in direct opposition to the righteous:

> The righteous man will flourish like the palm tree,
> He will grow like a cedar in Lebanon.
> Planted in the house of the Lord,
> They will flourish in the courts of our God.
> They will still yield fruit in old age;
> They shall be full of sap and very green,
> To declare that the Lord is upright;
> He is my rock, and there is no unrighteousness in Him. (vv. 12–15)

In a world full of injustice, this is how one is to rest on the seventh day as one awaits God's provision of the ultimate rest of the eighth day.

Since there is a final judgment to come for all, it is safe to assume that even believers will also be evaluated on that day. The difference between the believer's and the nonbeliever's judgment on that day is that believers in Christ will not be found wanting, not because they are inherently righteous but because their sins are paid for by Christ and they are clothed in the righteousness of Christ (2 Cor. 5:21).

Judgment of the Saints (Reward)

The desire for justice relates not only to the actions of the wicked but also to those of the righteous, especially with regard to their sacrifices for the sake of doing God's will. Very often, part of the mental calculus that goes into whether or not to obey God is the potential personal loss of benefits to oneself. And often such a loss results in the unwise choice of disobedience motivated by self-preservation.[15] The day of final judgment, therefore, is a reassurance to all that God will not forget their deeds on his behalf and that their labor in the Lord is not in vain (1 Cor. 15:58).

The apostle Paul depicts this day in Romans 2:5–11 as not only a day of judgment on the unrighteous but also a day of recompense for the righteous:

> But because of your stubbornness and unrepentant heart you are storing up wrath for yourself in the day of wrath and revelation of the righteous judgment of God, who will render to each person according to his deeds: to those who by perseverance in doing good seek for glory and honor and immortality, eternal life; but to those who are selfishly ambitious and do not obey the truth, but obey unrighteousness, wrath and indignation. There will be tribulation and distress for every soul of man who does evil, of the Jew first and also of the Greek, but glory and honor and peace to everyone who does good, to the Jew first and also to the Greek. For there is no partiality with God.

15. Any act of obedience to God demands that we change. But, as one source aptly observes, "When change involves real or potential loss, people hold on to what they have and resist the change." Heifetz, Grashow, and Linsky, *Practice of Adaptive Leadership*, 22.

Jesus is even more explicit in Matthew 19:28–30 about how the righteous will find their recompense or reward on that future day. He assures his followers,

> Truly I say to you, that you who have followed Me, in the regeneration when the Son of Man will sit on His glorious throne, you also shall sit upon twelve thrones, judging the twelve tribes of Israel. And everyone who has left houses or brothers or sisters or father or mother or children or farms for My name's sake, will receive many times as much, and will inherit eternal life. But many who are first will be last; and the last, first.

The final judgment thus turns the threat of personal loss in obedience to God on its head. It transforms the losses into a kind of delayed gratification. More than that, it becomes direction-setting for one's life, as seen in the life of Paul. He says that he has made it his "ambition whether at home or absent, to be pleasing to Him. For we must all appear before the judgment seat of Christ, so that each one may be recompensed for his deeds in the body, according to what he has done, whether good or bad" (2 Cor. 5:9–10).

Lest this is seen as a mere vulgar attempt to amass future rewards, the whole point of getting one's recompense is not personal future glory. The recompense is that we might glorify the One who has enabled us to live righteously and so receive the recompense. This is clearly seen in the heavenly scene where the twenty-four elders worship God using the crowns on their heads. Presumably, these crowns symbolize the reward they had received from God. Note what they do with their reward:

> The twenty-four elders will fall down before Him who sits on the throne, and will worship Him who lives forever and ever, and will cast their crowns before the throne, saying, "Worthy are You, our Lord and our God, to receive glory and honor and power; for You created all things, and because of Your will they existed, and were created." (Rev. 4:10–11)

Our reward, then, not only motivates us to live a life of present obedience and holiness but also becomes the basis of our eternal praise and worship of God, who has graciously given us the ability to live for him during our earthly existence.

3. Lack of Intimacy with God (Meaninglessness): God's Presence on Earth

Many times in our earthly existence, God is seen as not immediately accessible (Pss. 13; 42:1–5) or even hidden from us, whether because of our sin or our own mortality (Eccles. 3:11; Isa. 45:15). This condition has led to both frustration and a sense of despair and meaninglessness. The need to be in God's presence is especially acute when we are in dire need or oppressed by forces greater than us. The psalmist exemplifies this utter need to see God in times of distress in Psalm 42:1–3:

> As the deer pants for the water brooks,
> So my soul pants for You, O God.
> My soul thirsts for God, for the living God;
> When shall I come and appear before God?
> My tears have been my food day and night,
> While they say to me all day long, "Where is your God?"

In short, humanity yearns for the beatific vision—that is, the kind of communion we are created for as seen in the garden of Eden. So, the Creator of humankind has graciously accommodated humanity's unspoken desire by promising to make himself known. For this to happen, the world as we know it will have to be re-created.

God will re-create heaven and earth in order to make it possible for his dwelling to be with humanity and for access to him to become unhindered. In that future day, God himself will come down from heaven to tabernacle or dwell with his people on earth. Revelation 21:1–3 says, "Then I saw a new heaven and a new earth; for the first heaven and the first earth passed away, and there is no longer any sea. And I saw the holy city, new Jerusalem, coming down out of heaven from God, made ready as a bride adorned for her husband. And I heard a loud voice from the throne, saying, 'Behold, the tabernacle of God is among men, and He will dwell among them, and they shall be His people, and God Himself will be among them.'" The new Jerusalem coming down from heaven to earth depicts God coming down from heaven to be with his people.

Moreover, Revelation 21 goes on to make the observation that there is no "temple" and no heavenly bodies as we know them, such as the sun or the moon, to illuminate the world in that new existence (vv. 22–23).

What could these descriptions possibly mean? All these phenomena are consistent with the vision of a world where God is dwelling with his people. No temple is necessary, since God himself is personally present—no need for an intermediary such as a temple. And because God is with his people, his Shekinah glory will be enough to illuminate the world. There is no need for lesser luminaries. The Lamb of God will serve as the world's lamp.

On that day, God will no longer be "hidden" from his people. As in Eden, there will be a face-to-face communion with God. Indeed, even better than Eden, there will be an unbroken, permanent, face-to-face communion, removing any despair of not having his presence in our existence. The plea of Psalm 42 will at last be answered and will never have to be uttered again.

4. Pain and Suffering in Life (Hardships): Removal of Impediments to Human Flourishing

Because God is present with his people in that new world, the Bible shows that God will remove any impediment to life being lived to the fullest. All the curses that accompanied the fall of the old creation will be no more. Revelation 21:4 states that God will "wipe away every tear from their eyes; and there will no longer be any death; there will no longer be any mourning, or crying, or pain; the first things have passed away." One wonders exactly how God will do this.[16] But there is no denying that our past will no longer hinder the quality of our existence at that time.

Because nothing gets in the way of our full experience of life as God intended it, Revelation 22 clearly states, "There will no longer be any curse; and the throne of God and of the Lamb will be in it, and His bond-servants will serve Him" (v. 3). And since we will serve God wholeheartedly, this unhindered service to God will deepen the joy we experience in that future existence.

To be specific, the future life that God has planned for us is a life characterized by, at least, two distinct activities. First, it is characterized by worship of God and giving him glory forever. Revelation 21:24–27 says,

16. Some may think that God will do this by the deletion or erasure of bad memories and experiences we have had—a kind of mental amnesia. But it is probably better to see it as a conformity to God's memory and mental processes—that is, we will see our past events from his beneficent perspective (1 Cor. 13:11–12; 1 John 3:2). Thus, it is through the elevation of our mental processes, not their reduction, that God takes away the painful memories of our past life.

> The nations will walk by its light, and the kings of the earth will bring their glory into it. In the daytime (for there will be no night there) its gates will never be closed; and they will bring the glory and the honor of the nations into it; and nothing unclean, and no one who practices abomination and lying, shall ever come into it, but only those whose names are written in the Lamb's book of life.

Second, it involves the activity of reigning with Christ throughout eternity. Revelation 22:3–5 states, "There will no longer be any curse; and the throne of God and of the Lamb will be in it, and His bond-servants will serve Him; . . . and they will reign forever and ever." In many ways, this activity fulfills what God intended for humanity when he created them. They will be serving him as his coregents together with Christ in creation care and dominion.

Judgment of Satan

As part of the removal of any impediment to human flourishing, God will also render a final judgment on Satan. A driving force behind the present world's chaos and moral decay is Satan and his work of tempting humanity to sin. His influence is so vast in the world that he is given the shocking moniker of "the ruler of this world" (John 12:31; 16:11). Humanity, Scripture says, walks "according to the prince of the power of the air, of the spirit that is now working in the sons of disobedience" (Eph. 2:2). Clearly, part of the human yearning for a better world cannot come to fruition without arresting Satan's impact on humanity.

In that future day, Scripture shows that Satan, the one who caused humanity to fall into sin in the garden and has since been instrumental for humanity's enslavement to sin, will be judged. He will be rendered ineffective, sent to destruction, as Revelation 20:10 describes: "And the devil who deceived them was thrown into the lake of fire and brimstone, where the beast and the false prophet are also; and they will be tormented day and night forever and ever." Having been rendered inoperative, his influence in the world will be forever nonexistent.

This defeat is prophesied in Genesis 3:15, sometimes called the *protevangelium* (the first gospel), which foretold in veiled form the coming victory of Christ over Satan at the cross. It states,

> And I will put enmity
> Between you and the woman,
> And between your seed and her seed;
> He shall bruise you on the head,
> And you shall bruise him on the heel.

What is merely foreshadowed in the Old Testament, however, is made abundantly clear in the New Testament at the coming of Jesus Christ. Colossians 2:15 states, "When He had disarmed the rulers and authorities [at the cross], He made a public display of them, having triumphed over them through Him [Christ]."

So, believers are no longer enslaved to Satan. They need not give in to sin. But because he is still at loose and his influence is still evident in the world, believers must remain vigilant. They must engage him by resisting his temptations and put on God's provision of the "armor of God" (Eph. 6:11, 13) lest they suffer unnecessary losses. Unfortunately, many believers even today do experience this tragic defeat. But the reassurance of the Bible is that in the final judgment, Satan and his minions will be judged and thrown into the lake of fire, and their influence will be no more. As Paul promises in Romans 16:20, "The God of peace will soon crush Satan under your feet."

The Means to Appropriating the Eighth Day of Creation: The Messiah

Aside from the specificity of Christian eschatological hope, a second difference from other worldviews is the means by which it is appropriated. For Christians, the means of appropriating God's future hope for us is God's promise of a coming Messiah. God had promised King David that one of his sons would be designated as king in his place. And this Davidic descendant will reign on his throne forever. In 2 Samuel 7:11–13 we read,

> The LORD also declares to you [David] that the LORD will make a house for you. When your days are complete and you lie down with your fathers, I will raise up your descendant after you, who will come forth from you, and I will establish his kingdom. He shall build a house for My name, and I will establish the throne of his kingdom forever.

God's promise to David is connected to the eighth day of creation. For the establishment of the Messiah's kingdom on earth is actually the means by which God will bring about the future new creation. In Daniel 2:44, it is described as a kingdom that "the God of heaven will set up" and as "a kingdom which will never be destroyed" and will "put an end to all these kingdoms, but it will itself endure forever." To be more specific, according to Daniel 7, God will hand this everlasting kingdom to a messianic figure who is called the "Son of Man." A magnificent heavenly scene of this enthronement is shown in Daniel 7:13–14:

> I kept looking in the night visions,
> And behold, with the clouds of heaven
> One like a Son of Man was coming,
> And He came up to the Ancient of Days
> And was presented before Him.
> And to Him was given dominion,
> Glory and a kingdom,
> That all the peoples, nations and men of every language
> Might serve Him.
> His dominion is an everlasting dominion
> Which will not pass away;
> And His kingdom is one
> Which will not be destroyed.

To enter into this coming kingdom of God in the future, one must, therefore, look to the Son of Man. He is the access to it. Indeed, he is the same figure as the one coming in King David's line and who will reign on his throne.

Who is this Son of Man who will inherit the kingdom of God? The New Testament reveals to us that it is none other than Jesus Christ. When Jesus starts his earthly ministry, the message that he proclaims is that of the kingdom of God (Matt. 3:1–2; Mark 1:14–15). And one of his favorite self-descriptions is the title Son of Man. The following are three instances of such self-designation tying him explicitly to Daniel 7's prophecy:

> Jesus said to him, "The foxes have holes and the birds of the air have nests, but the Son of Man has nowhere to lay His head." (Matt. 8:20)

> "But so that you may know that the Son of Man has authority on earth to forgive sins"—then He said to the paralytic, "Get up, pick up your bed and go home." (Matt. 9:6)

> He answered and said to them . . . "Just as Jonah was three days and three nights in the belly of the sea monster, so will the Son of Man be three days and three nights in the heart of the earth." (Matt. 12:39–40)

And so he invites those who are in need of this greater rest that only God can give to put their trust and hope in him.

The incarnation of Jesus is not only a confirmation that he is the designated Messiah and, therefore, the key to appropriating the promise of the eighth day. In addition, because he is God (the second member of the Trinity), the incarnation ensures that our faith allegiance to him will never become idolatrous, competing with humanity's ultimate devotion to the one true God alone (Deut. 6:4–5). As Reinhold Niebuhr notes, this seems to be the problem of many human leaders who promise utopia to the masses. "Evil is introduced into history by the very effort of men to solve this [vexing existential] problem by their own resources," for "'false eternals' of human pride" are often introduced, which makes matters worse for humanity.[17] One can only think of political figures such as Hitler, Mao, Stalin, and others who promised such utopian societies to satisfy the eschatological yearnings of the masses but did so at the expense of propping themselves up to become idols. But the Christian hope, which is grounded in the divinity of Jesus Christ, is safeguarded from such idolatrous claims. For as Scripture says, this Christian hope is based on the fact that "God was in Christ reconciling the world to Himself" (2 Cor. 5:19).

The Nature of the Eighth Day of Creation Providence: Anticipatory

Unlike the seventh day of creation, where human participation is involved, the eighth day of creation is purely the work of God. In short, it is by grace. Scripture delineates the requirement and the effect of such waiting and hoping in the future God has prepared for his people. Hebrews 11:1–3 shows the correlation of hope and true faith:

17. Niebuhr, *Nature and Destiny of Man*, 287.

> Now faith is the assurance of things hoped for, the conviction of things not seen. For by it the men of old gained approval. By faith we understand that the worlds were prepared by the word of God, so that what is seen was not made out of things which are visible.

Moreover, Romans 8:24–25 states,

> For in hope we have been saved, but hope that is seen is not hope; for who hopes for what he already sees? But if we hope for what we do not see, with perseverance we wait eagerly for it.

Thus, the human role is one of faithful anticipation for God to make his move. This kind of hopeful faith in him (and not relying so much on busy work) is at the heart of what it means to follow Christ and what God required of those who would reap from his eschatological provision. Note this exchange between Jesus and his disciples:

> [Jesus said,] "Do not work for the food which perishes, but for the food which endures to eternal life, which the Son of Man will give to you, for on Him the Father, God, has set His seal." Therefore they said to Him, "What shall we do, so that we may work the works of God?" Jesus answered and said to them, "This is the work of God, that you believe in Him whom He has sent." (John 6:27–29)

At first glance, such waiting and hoping may seem counterproductive. But it isn't. For the One who became incarnate and the One in whom we believe will not just stand idly by in our life. He will command and he will lead us—although everything begins at the point of quiet reception of him and his purposes in our hearts. This quiet reception of Christ's hope is what directs and energizes the Christian's life. Emil Brunner insightfully says,

> Faith is first quiet, peace, rest; the turmoil of the soul is silenced; the strain of striving has come to an end, for as a believer one *has* and *is*. . . . This quiet and peace, this having and being, however, is not that of the mystic who passively enjoys heaven upon earth. It is rather the call of the Lord of hosts who is constantly recruiting men for his army, the *ecclesia militans*. He who has taken the inner fortress of your soul, i.e., your Ego, will not stop there but

> will take you with him to conquer the world. The eschatological substance of faith works itself out in supremely aggressive action in the world.[18]

This led C. S. Lewis to make the following observation regarding Christian hope:

> If you read history you will find that the Christians who did most for the present world are just the ones that thought the most of the next. The Apostles themselves, who set on foot the conversion of the Roman Empire, the great men who built up the Middle Ages, the English Evangelicals who abolished the Slave Trade, all left their mark on Earth, precisely because their minds were occupied with Heaven. It is since Christians have largely ceased to think of the other world that they have become so ineffective in this. Aim at Heaven and you'll get the earth "thrown in": aim at earth and you'll get neither.[19]

The Value of the Eighth-Day Providence

Returning to Wellington's victory at Waterloo against Napoleon's troops, we see clearly that the reinforcement from Marshal Blücher and his Prussian troops was indispensable. So, in answer to the question "Could Wellington have won the Battle of Waterloo without the Prussians?" one military expert astutely said, "Wrong question. He'd never have fought the battle if he hadn't known that the Prussians were on the way."[20] How true! Any wise general would not and could not persevere in fighting an intense battle without having confident hope of reinforcement. Life is a battle—bigger than Waterloo—and like Wellington, we cannot persevere without hope (real and assured hope).

As Billy Graham said, "One of the best ways to get rid of discouragement is to remember that Christ is coming again. The most thrilling, glorious truth in all the world is the Second Coming of Jesus Christ."[21] No wonder that among the final words of the Bible we read, "He who testifies to these things says, 'Yes, I am coming quickly.' Amen. Come, Lord Jesus" (Rev. 22:20).

18. Brunner, *Theology of Crisis*, 84.

19. Lewis, *Mere Christianity*, 134.

20. "Great British Commanders: Arthur Wellesley—1st Duke of Wellington," YouTube video, 22:28, posted by Prince Corsica, July 31, 2018, https://youtu.be/nuJZU-N6sEE.

21. Billy Graham, "Encouragement," Billy Graham Evangelistic Association, July 11, 2023, https://billygraham.org/devotion/encouragement.

6

God's Providence in the "Already" of the Eighth Day of Creation, Part 1

Present Impact in Relation to the Triune God

> The . . . Church of Christ is spiritually unable to stand against the rapid changes that take place around her because she has not learned to view history from the perspective of the reign of Christ. For that reason, she thinks of the events of her own time in entirely secular terms.
>
> —Hendrikus Berkhof, *Christ: The Meaning of History*

Living in Tomorrowland Today

One of the benefits of growing up in Southern California was the close proximity of Disneyland to where I lived. Whenever the opportunity arose (and the ticket price was right), my family and I would spend the day at Mickey Mouse's theme park. My favorite section in Disneyland was Tomorrowland because it fired up my imagination of what the future might be. Somehow, it also made me feel that a bit of the future had been brought to the present for me to experience. On a good day I could even sense that I was actually transported into the future itself. Walt Disney would have been happy to know that Tomorrowland had such an effect on me. For that was exactly what he intended Tomorrowland to be and do to those who visit there.[1]

How did Walt Disney and his group of Imagineers do it? It is no secret that they took the latest scientific discoveries and futuristic projections and replicated them in Tomorrowland to the best of their ability. And if they couldn't do it themselves, Disneyland staff invited technology companies to put on display their latest research and development. But a very important ingredient to the futuristic experience involves the element of audience participation. Whether implicitly or explicitly, Tomorrowland encourages visitors to let their imagination further guide them in experiencing all that they see and feel in their surroundings. There is no doubt that a healthy dose of "suspension of disbelief" (i.e., faith in what Disneyland puts on display) is involved in order for the simple as well as complicated props to give patrons a sense of the future. By doing these things, Disneyland ushers in a little bit of the future for their patrons to experience. So, on a good day patrons find themselves somehow transported into the bright future that Walt Disney and his Imagineers would have us embrace. No wonder it's called the "magic kingdom" and the "happiest place on earth." For we all leave Disneyland a little more optimistic about the future than when we first arrived because we've been to the future and back.

Disneyland's Tomorrowland is an imperfect parallel to the eighth day of creation. After promising us a coming glorious future, God is not simply interested in portraying it to us with words. He wants us also to experience it today (indeed, to the point of being transported, as it were, to the future he created for us). His purpose is that we might have a hopeful outlook not only on the future but also on our present existence no matter what circumstance we're in. As a result, humanity can be empowered to truly be God's junior partners in the care of his creation.

In theological parlance, this process of drawing upon God's completed future and bringing aspects of it to the present is called "prolepsis."[2] Indeed, this is not a novel idea but rather one that the New Testament

1. In 1958, related to his vision for a Tomorrowland, Walt Disney said, "We step into the future and find fantastic atomic-powered machines working for us. The world is unified and peaceful, outer space is the new frontier. We walk for a time among the strange mechanical wonders of tomorrow, and then blast off on a rocket to the moon." Williams, *How to Be like Walt*, 240.

2. See Pannenberg, *Theology*, 69; Grenz, *Reason for Hope*, 117; and Peters, *God*.

church practiced. It is bound up in the concept of the "already and not yet" of the kingdom of God.

While there are similarities, there are also dissimilarities between Tomorrowland and the eighth day of creation's proleptic approach to the future. For one, Tomorrowland's portrayal of the future is based on human scientific discoveries or innovations. In that sense, it is both limited and fallible. But the future from which believers understand the eighth day of creation comes from God himself. Therefore, it is settled and trustworthy. It is one in which we can *objectively* build a meaningful and hope-filled life today.

The biggest difference between Tomorrowland and the eighth day of creation is the means by which the future can be experienced today. In the case of the former, it is the patron's suspension of disbelief or faith in what Disneyland is presenting. But in the case of the latter, it is faith in God's divine revelation of a future that he promised. Both require faith in the one who is portraying the future—if the future is to be experienced proleptically today. But the kind of faith that one exercises to enjoy Tomorrowland is temporal in nature. In other words, it is true only while one is in the theme park, but it does not persist throughout the person's life. As an example, we put on 3D spectacles in order to enjoy a ride or a feature in Tomorrowland. But the moment the attraction is over, and certainly after we leave Disneyland, we also leave the 3D spectacles behind. The only thing that remains is the memory of what we encountered. It is not the same, however, with faith in God's proleptic future of the eighth day of creation. To experience it, one must not only remain in that faith but also, indeed, grow in that faith in Christ by turning it into love for him. It is at that point that the fullness of the proleptic future of the eighth day of salvation can be fully experienced in a meaningful way. If this nascent faith is grown and developed into an undying love for Christ, then the proleptic encounter of the eighth day of creation need not just be momentary but rather becomes a permanent reality for the Christian even while he or she awaits the full consummation of all that God has promised on the eighth day of creation.

As one can quickly see, though, such faith-turned-love cannot be based on human ability. It has to be divinely energized. So, it is by God's grace alone. To put it in trinitarian terms, it is God the Father who made such a wonderful providence possible through the agency of the Son (Jesus

Christ) and the Holy Spirit. As Kevin Vanhoozer eloquently puts it, "Divine providence is less a matter of God's 'strong right hand' than of the Father's *two* hands (i.e., Son and Spirit)—in a word, triune authorship. . . . [This means:] *the Father rules by speaking Christ through the Spirit into the minds and hearts of the faithful.*"[3]

Five Ways for Appropriating Proleptically God's Eighth Day of Creation (Nos. 1–2)

Thus, as we consider how the eighth day of creation can be accessed proleptically, it stands to reason that it involves the Father's two hands: Jesus Christ and the Holy Spirit. Within the general rubric of the Son and the Spirit, there are at least five ways in which, by his grace, God has providentially given us the means by which we can benefit proleptically from the future that he has in store for us. One can think of them as a kind of means of grace for appropriating proleptically God's eighth day of creation.

The following are the five ways:

1. through the incarnation of Jesus Christ
2. through the indwelling Holy Spirit
3. through the believer's personal narrative in Christ
4. through the communion of the saints (the church)
5. through synchronizing to God's time

The first two ways will be discussed in this chapter. They deal with the proleptic impact that the eighth day of creation has on our present relationship with the triune God. The other three will be discussed in the following chapter. And they deal with the proleptic impact that the eighth day of creation has on our present relationship with the world at large.

1. Through the Incarnation of Jesus Christ

Jesus Christ is God who took upon himself human nature (the incarnation) for the purpose of representing fallen humanity before God

3. Vanhoozer, *Remythologizing Theology*, 367, 376.

the Father. He is God the Father's gift to humanity so that, through his theanthropic being and work, he might accomplish everything that God required of humanity, which we were unable to fulfill.

Note that Jesus is described as the last Adam in 1 Corinthians 15:45–49, where Paul says,

> So also it is written, "The first man, Adam, became a living soul." The last Adam became a life-giving spirit. . . . The first man is from the earth, earthy; the second man is from heaven. . . . Just as we have borne the image of the earthy, we will also bear the image of the heavenly.

And, again, Christ is shown in Romans 5:17–19 as the one who alone obeyed God on behalf of all humanity:

> For if by the transgression of the one, death reigned through the one, much more those who receive the abundance of grace and of the gift of righteousness will reign in life through the One, Jesus Christ. So then as through one transgression there resulted condemnation to all men, even so through one act of righteousness there resulted justification of life to all men. For as through the one man's disobedience the many were made sinners, even so through the obedience of the One the many will be made righteous.

Rightly did Karl Barth characterize Christ as "our representative before God."[4] Dietrich Bonhoeffer aptly puts it this way: "It is implicit in the New Testament statement concerning the incarnation of God in Christ that all men are taken up, enclosed and borne within the body of Christ and that this is just what the congregation of the faithful are to make known to the world by their words and by their lives."[5]

Everything about the being of Jesus Christ—his origin, birth, life, death, resurrection, ascension, and return to reign on earth—points us to what

4. Barth, *Prayer*, 34.

5. Bonhoeffer, *Ethics*, 72. Others in church history have expressed it in terms of recapitulation. Irenaeus of Lyons wrote, "He has therefore, in His work of recapitulation, summed up all things, both waging war against our enemy, and crushing him who had at the beginning led us away captives in Adam. . . . And therefore does the Lord profess Himself to be the Son of man, comprising in Himself that original man out of whom the woman was fashioned . . . in order that, as our species went down to death through a vanquished man, so we may ascend to life again through a victorious one; and as through a man death received the palm [of victory] against us, so again by a man we may receive the palm against death." Irenaeus, *Against Heresies* 5.21.1 (*ANF* 1:548–49).

God has in store for us on the eighth day of creation. Indeed, more than that, a faith relationship with Jesus Christ is not only humanity's pathway to God's future blessings but also the very means of experiencing those future blessings in our present day and age. He is the key to the prolepsis of the eighth day of creation.

Admittedly, the notion that Christ's being or personhood can be a way for us to enter into that eighth-day blessing today is not an easy concept to grasp. But it is not impossible. To experience the prolepsis of the eighth-day creation, we have to expand or elaborate our understanding of Christ as the last Adam.[6] One way is to see Jesus Christ as possessing "incorporative power" in his being. R. R. Reno states,

> Jesus saves because his identity "for us" has incorporative power, which allows Jesus to stand in our place. "While we were still weak," writes Paul, "at the right time Christ died for the ungodly" (Rom. 5:6). Furthermore, Jesus' incorporative power draws us into a continuous form of life. "We have been buried with him by baptism into death," Paul teaches, "so that, just as Christ was raised from the dead by the glory of the Father, so we too might walk in newness of life" (6:4).[7]

He goes on to explain, citing Thomas Aquinas:

> As head of the Church, Christ shows himself to possess this potency as an incorporative, not individual, power, which is entirely fitting, for Jesus is the power of God's "for us," not "for himself." Because of this incorporative power, Aquinas concludes, "there is the same relation between Christ's deeds for himself and his members, as there is between what another man does in the state of grace and himself."[8]

Let me illustrate. On July 16, 1969, the crew of the spacecraft Apollo 11, consisting of astronauts Neil Armstrong, Buzz Aldrin, and Michael

6. In addition to being the last Adam, another biblical way to conceptualize of Jesus as possessing "incorporative power" is his standing as king or a monarch, which is what the title Christ or Messiah signifies. As a potentate, he is naturally someone who has the power to bring his people within his aegis. Seen this way, the name Jesus the Christ would naturally connote such a power, especially for someone living during the time of the early church. It is up to modern Christianity to rediscover this connection.

7. Reno, *Redemptive Change*, 212–13.

8. Reno, *Redemptive Change*, 227, citing Aquinas, *Summa theologiae* III.48.1.

Collins, landed on the moon. It was a historic and spectacular feat not just for the United States but for all of humankind, as it was the first time that humanity had set foot on the moon. Upon landing, the astronauts planted a US flag and placed a plaque on the surface of the moon stating, "Here men from the planet Earth first set foot upon the moon, July 1969 A.D. We came in peace for all mankind." Apollo 11 then safely returned to Earth on July 24, 1969. From there, the crew went on a tour around the world sharing their tremendous experience in outer space. According to astronaut Michael Collins, "I was amazed that everywhere we went people would say, 'We, we did it!' You and me, the inhabitants of this wonderful earth, we did it!"[9] Collins added, "Instead of saying, 'You Americans did it,' they said, 'We did it.'"[10]

Surely, the people whom the astronauts visited around the world knew who financed the Apollo 11 flight and whose flag was planted on the moon. Moreover, they were well aware that they did not leave planet Earth to go to the moon. But their perspective was bigger than national boundaries or the normal concept of the self at that time. The people of the world saw in these three astronauts their human representatives on the moon. It can be fairly said that the astronauts possessed an incorporative power to take upon themselves the people of the world so that what they did in that historic event transcended their individual achievements. When they walked the surface of the moon, they incorporated the people of the earth unto themselves and carried within them the hopes and dreams of all humanity since the beginning of time. In a sense, the astronauts in 1969 have become bigger than themselves and incorporated the entire human race. Such is the case with Jesus Christ in the incarnation. The exception is that Christ's representative and incorporative power is infinitely more significant than the act of landing on the moon. So, to truly appreciate the significance of the incarnation, one must see Jesus Christ in the same worldwide impact manner. His becoming a man is "for us" humanity in order that the blessings of the eighth day might be ours. And, indeed, he has secured them "for us" within himself.

9. "50th Anniversary of the Moon Landing," YouTube video, 4:37, posted by GoogleDoodles, July 18, 2019, https://youtu.be/uzbquKCqEQY.

10. "Behind the Doodle: 50th Anniversary of the Moon Landing," YouTube video, 3:39, posted by GoogleDoodles, July 18, 2019, https://youtu.be/kKTZouDScj4.

The Requirement of Faith

The way to appropriate what Jesus Christ has done for us in his incarnation is to simply but sincerely accept it by faith. The apostle Paul plainly states in Romans 5:1–2, "Therefore, having been justified by faith, we have peace with God through our Lord Jesus Christ, through whom also we have obtained our introduction by faith into this grace in which we stand." And, again, in Ephesians 3:12, he stresses the role of faith as requisite to enter into this reality: "We have boldness and confident access [to God the Father] through faith in Him [Jesus Christ]." Paraphrasing Paul's teaching on faith, Emil Brunner puts it in this provocative way:

> God cannot be known by theoretical reason but must be comprehended by an act of decision. The word of God can be answered only by the yea of decision and not by the yea of a theoretical conviction. . . . So faith is the act of acceptance, i.e., decision. . . . When we believe in the word of God alone and therefore in the promise of the future we have entered the way of salvation. This assurance of the future, through faith, is present salvation.[11]

Going back to the illustration of Apollo 11, we noted that the astronauts' feat may have represented all of humanity. But the accomplishment of landing on the moon holds no personal meaning or significance to a person whom the astronauts represented there unless that person is willing to accept by faith the intended act of representation. Thus, faith on the part of those who did not go to the moon is essential if they are to appropriate for themselves what the astronauts did on behalf of humanity there. Such is also the kind of faith needed to form a nexus between Jesus and those for whom he came to live out the incarnation and fulfill its salvific mission. And it is through this same kind of faith that one experiences proleptically today Christ's eighth-day creation work on their behalf.

In many ways, this emphasis on the necessity of faith in Jesus Christ has always been the Christian message of *solus Christus* and *sola fide*, with which many Christians are familiar. Such a doctrine is so common that it is almost taken for granted in the Christian community. But if it is so common, why is it that those who believe or have faith in Christ do not

11. Brunner, *Theology of Crisis*, 63.

always experience proleptically the blessings of the eighth day of creation? I suggest that the reason is that one important ingredient is missing.

The Requirement of Faith Transposed to Love

Faith in the incarnate Christ as the last Adam who came "for us" may be a necessary first step. But it cannot be the last step if we are to experience the realities of the eighth day of creation in Christ. Indeed, faith in Christ must grow to become love for Christ. It is this faith in Christ turned into love for Christ that is necessary for the proleptic experience of the eighth day of creation on a daily and moment-by-moment basis in our current fallen existence prior to that future glorious day.

The premier example of someone in the Bible who not only came to Christ by faith but also began to live a new life characterized by the eighth day of creation is the apostle Paul. He clearly taught the proleptic living of the future blessings of Christ is for today, as seen in 2 Corinthians 5:16–17.

> Therefore from now on we recognize no one according to the flesh; even though we have known Christ according to the flesh, yet now we know Him in this way no longer. Therefore if anyone is in Christ, he is a new creature; the old things passed away; behold, new things have come.

He did not just teach this truth; he lived it and showed it in the way he lived it out. Galatians 2:20 captures well how he did it. Paul describes himself in Galatians 2:20 this way: "I have been crucified with Christ; and it is no longer I who live, but Christ lives in me; and the life which I now live in the flesh I live by faith in the Son of God, who loved me and gave Himself up for me." Notice that all of Paul's earthly existence is lived "by faith in the Son of God." And this kind of living is no shallow religious piety. He says that it is a life no longer lived for himself but for Christ. It is tantamount to a life being crucified with Christ. But what is his motivation? What transforms his faith in Christ into an intense devotion to him? The answer is found in the last part of verse 20, where he describes Christ as "the Son of God, who loved me and gave Himself up for me." At first glance, it seems like a throwaway line. But upon closer examination, it is the dynamo that sets Paul's faith into turbo action. In short, it is the love of Christ for him that turns his faith into devotion. Herein is the principle at hand: faith in Christ nourished constantly by the incarnation love of

Christ will transform the believer to respond in kind. When that happens, the believer also experiences the proleptic blessings of the eighth day of creation through Jesus Christ.[12] This is what we witness in the life of the apostle Paul.

Dietrich Bonhoeffer gives a wonderful description of this transformation that proleptically allows us to experience the eighth day of creation today in Christ:

> Christ followers always have his image before their eyes, and in its light all other images are screened from their sight. It penetrates into the depths of their being, fills them, and makes them more and more like their Master. The image of Jesus Christ impresses itself in daily communion on the image of the disciple. No follower of Jesus can contemplate his image in a spirit of cold detachment. That image has the power to transform our lives, and if we surrender ourselves utterly to him, we cannot help bearing his image ourselves. . . . If we contemplate the image of the glorified Christ we shall be made like unto it, just as by contemplating the image of Christ crucified we are conformed to his death. We shall be drawn into his image and identified with his form, and become a reflection of him. That reflection of his glory will shine forth in us even in this life even as we share his agony and bear his cross. Our life will then be a progress from knowledge to knowledge, from glory to glory, to an ever closer conformity with the image of the son of God.[13]

Going back once more to the Apollo 11 illustration, we find it heartening to see how many people around the earth embrace (by faith) the astronauts' moon landing as representing them. But it is probably safe to say that the astronauts would not also represent them in many other things that they do. Most people would not see themselves living vicariously through all of the experiences of the astronauts. For that kind of faith to develop, it must evolve into an affectional attachment to the astronauts. The initial faith must be transposed into love and expanded into all areas of life. So when it comes to believers' faith in Christ, that is exactly the kind of faith transposition that God wants to develop in us so that through our deep and sincere affection for Christ we can experience the proleptic blessings of the eighth day of creation.

12. See Piper, *What Is Saving Faith?*, 170–71.
13. Bonhoeffer, *Cost of Discipleship*, 298, 303.

2. *Through the Indwelling Holy Spirit*

Aside from incorporating us to himself, Jesus Christ has also given us the Holy Spirit. Through the gift of the Holy Spirit, who is the third member of the Trinity and is the very source that empowered Jesus's earthly ministry, Jesus Christ made it possible for those who believe in him to proleptically experience the eschatological life that God the Father has promised in Scripture. If Jesus Christ is the embodiment of the eschatological kingdom to come, then our reception of the Holy Spirit is a sure sign that we have come to share proleptically the glorious future manifestation of the kingdom life today.

The apostle Paul confirms this understanding when he asserts that when we believe in the gospel of Jesus Christ, we are "sealed in Him with the Holy Spirit of promise, who is given as a pledge of our inheritance, with a view to the redemption of God's own possession, to the praise of His glory" (Eph. 1:13–14). The Greek word for "pledge" is *arrabōn*, which means "down payment, earnest, surety, guarantee"[14] of the promise of our inheritance.[15] Whatever is true of the whole (completed or fulfilled promise of future inheritance) is true of the part (the present down payment or pledge of the Holy Spirit). Thus, as God's *arrabōn*, the Holy Spirit in the believer gives us a foretaste of all the future glory that God promised. Practically and experientially speaking, the Holy Spirit gives believers access to the future blessings of the eighth day of creation in our present time in the following ways:

- the fruit of the Spirit
- the guidance of the Spirit
- the filling of the Spirit
- the empowerment of the Spirit

The Fruit of the Spirit

The fruit of the Spirit is the inner transformation that comes from the very indwelling of the Holy Spirit in the life of the believer. Galatians

14. See also Paul's similar usage in 2 Cor. 1:22.

15. This could be a reference to either that God will further demonstrate to us in the future that we are his precious inheritance or that God will give us the remainder of his promised inheritance to us. Grammatically and contextually, the former view is preferred. But it does not change the force of the statement that the Holy Spirit is the present assurance of that future reality.

5:22–23 states, "The fruit of the Spirit is love, joy, peace, patience, kindness, goodness, faithfulness, gentleness, self-control; against such things there is no law." The reception of the Holy Spirit upon conversion to Christ brings about these fruits of moral virtues that will one day be seen in abundance and consistently on the eighth day of creation. But they are available now to the believer in some measure through the Spirit. This phenomenon fulfills the Old Testament prophecy of the coming new covenant whereby God said,

> I will put My law within them and on their heart I will write it; and I will be their God, and they shall be My people. They will not teach again, each man his neighbor and each man his brother, saying, "Know the LORD," for they will all know Me, from the least of them to the greatest of them. (Jer. 31:33–34)

> Moreover, I will give you a new heart and put a new spirit within you; and I will remove the heart of stone from your flesh and give you a heart of flesh. I will put My Spirit within you and cause you to walk in My statutes, and you will be careful to observe My ordinances. (Ezek. 36:26–27)

It is important to note, though, that the teaching on the fruit of the Spirit does not say that the transformation will be immediate or completed in this present lifetime, but that it will and, indeed, should be discernible in the life of the believer over the course of his or her life.[16] Such is God's gracious proleptic provision in Christ through the Spirit.

The Guidance of the Spirit

The indwelling Holy Spirit of Christ comes not simply as a mere potential for inner transformation but as an unmistakable persuasive influence that guides believers into all truth and righteousness. In Galatians 5:16, Paul exhorts believers to "walk by the Spirit," for he is the indwelling divine presence that leads and guides them. Indeed, it is imperative that they do so. "For all who are being led by the Spirit of God, these are

16. This is where the bearing of the fruit of the Spirit coincides with the teaching of progressive sanctification, which states that the believer's becoming more and more like Christ does not happen overnight but progressively in the course of the believer's life, sometimes even in fits and starts. But there is no denying where the trajectory of the believer's life is heading.

sons of God" (Rom. 8:14). Such a responsive practice of attending to the Spirit's guidance in one's life ultimately leads to an existence of "pleasing" God and, thus, to "life and peace" (8:6–8). And these are some of the manifestations of the eighth day of creation that can be experienced in the life of the believer today. As Paul says in Romans 14:17, "For the kingdom of God is not eating and drinking, but righteousness and peace and joy in the Holy Spirit."

If on the eighth day of creation the presence of God will be evident everywhere in the life of believers, then the indwelling Holy Spirit makes the presence of the Father and the Son evident to believers today. And this is especially discernible in the case where we obey the guidance of the Holy Spirit even in the face of danger. In Jesus's counsel to his disciples before commissioning them to their perilous missionary journey, we see a beautiful work of the Holy Spirit couched in trinitarian terms. First, Jesus says to them, "But when they hand you over, do not worry about how or what you are to say; for it will be given you in that hour what you are to say. For it is not you who speak, but it is the Spirit of your Father who speaks in you" (Matt. 10:19–20). This instruction underscores the Father's presence through the Spirit. But later, as though to emphasize his own presence to help in the believer's predicament, Jesus says that the same Spirit's guidance is also a manifestation of his presence at that very moment. He says,

> Therefore do not fear them, for there is nothing concealed that will not be revealed, or hidden that will not be known. What I tell you in the darkness, speak in the light; and what you hear whispered in your ear, proclaim upon the housetops. Do not fear those who kill the body but are unable to kill the soul; but rather fear Him who is able to destroy both soul and body in hell. (Matt. 10:26–28)

So, the Spirit's guidance is the manifestation of both the Father's and the Son's presence whenever we seek to follow his guidance.

The Filling of the Spirit

As the indwelling and the guidance of the Holy Spirit connote the divine initiative, the Bible also speaks of the filling of the Holy Spirit as a related means of experiencing the eighth day of creation proleptically. Filling of the Holy Spirit entails the believer allowing the indwelling Holy Spirit, who is guiding, to have more and more control of the believer, not in a sense of being coerced but of loving self-surrender to the gracious third person of the Trinity. Paul writes in Ephesians 5:18–21,

> Do not get drunk with wine, for that is dissipation, but be filled with the Spirit, speaking to one another in psalms and hymns and spiritual songs, singing and making melody with your heart to the Lord; always giving thanks for all things in the name of our Lord Jesus Christ to God, even the Father; and be subject to one another in the fear of Christ.

Instead of being controlled by wine, which leads to worthless drunkenness, believers are exhorted to be "filled" with the Spirit of Christ in the same manner that a drunkard is filled with wine; thereby their lives should exhibit the influence of such Christ-centered filling. The command, therefore, calls for believers to attend to the presence of the Holy Spirit in their lives guiding them to the proper action. In Philippians 2:12–13, Paul characterizes this attention to the inner working of God through the Holy Spirit with this sober counsel: "So then, my beloved, just as you have always obeyed, not as in my presence only, but now much more in my absence, work out your salvation with fear and trembling; for it is God who is at work in you, both to will and to work for His good pleasure." Thus, the believer is not passive in this process of being filled with Spirit, which is the way to a consistent experience of the proleptic eighth day of creation. The believer must actively respond to the Holy Spirit within.

In a helpful parallel text, Colossians 3:16, Paul not only shows us what being filled with the Spirit means but also points us to the means of being filled by the Spirit: "Let the word of Christ richly dwell within you, with all wisdom teaching and admonishing one another with psalms and hymns and spiritual songs, singing with thankfulness in your hearts to God." The key to this infilling is not some esoteric activity but rather is the very initial activity of believing in Christ, except that now it is intensified in letting Christ's word "richly dwell within you." It will naturally lead to the kind of worshipful, Christ-centered lifestyle characteristic of the future aspects of the eighth day of creation. All the comfort and intimacy that we desire of the Lord in the eschaton, therefore, can be experienced in miniature today through this filling of the Spirit.

The Empowerment of the Spirit

Throughout the infilling process, as Philippians 2:12–13 shows, we are not alone in doing the work of yielding to the ways of Christ; the Holy Spirit even then is working in our interior life to enable us to do it. We are enabled to consistently break free from the chains of sin within the course of our earthly walk with the Lord so as to experience a measure of victory over sin's influence in our life. Such enablement connotes the empowerment of the Holy Spirit in the life of the believer so that he or she can follow Christ and in so doing experience the eternal life that he came to bestow on us on the eighth day of creation. As noted, on that future day, there will be no more sea (i.e., evil or sin). That kind of glorious experience can be experienced in some sense even today through the Holy Spirit's empowerment.

It is this mighty working of the Holy Spirit in the life of the believer that marked the era of the new covenant under the aegis of the Messiah. In this way, John the Baptist points out correctly what the Messiah would do: "As for me, I baptize you with water; but One is coming who is mightier than I, and I am not fit to untie the thong of His sandals; He will baptize you with the Holy Spirit and fire'" (Luke 3:16). Jesus himself affirms John the Baptist's understanding of the work of the Messiah. After his return from successfully overcoming Satan's temptation in the wilderness for forty days, Jesus enters the synagogue in Capernaum and makes this bold proclamation in reading from the prophet Isaiah:

> The Spirit of the Lord is upon Me,
> Because He anointed Me to preach the gospel to the poor.
> He has sent Me to proclaim release to the captives,
> And recovery of sight to the blind,
> To set free those who are oppressed,
> To proclaim the favorable year of the Lord. (Luke 4:18–19)

But this Spirit of God within him is not confined only to his own being. In a breathtaking statement, Jesus says, "Truly, truly, I say to you, he who believes in Me, the works that I do, he will do also; and greater works than these he will do; because I go to the Father" (John 14:12). And ever since the day of Pentecost, the church (the assembly of those who believe in Christ) has been marked by this supernatural empowerment of the

Holy Spirit that comes from Jesus Christ. It is safe to say that the New Testament does not shy away from expecting that the supernatural power of the Holy Spirit will be at work in the life of the individual believer as well as the lives of believers assembled. As such, therefore, the writer to the Hebrews describes those who have experienced the power of the Holy Spirit as those who have tasted "the powers of the age to come" (Heb. 6:5).

Thus, Paul could write this to the believers in Thessalonica, assuring them that the gospel message they heard and, therefore, their conversion are genuinely from God: "knowing, brethren beloved by God, His choice of you; for our gospel did not come to you in word only, but also in power and in the Holy Spirit and with full conviction" (1 Thess. 1:4–5). Such proof, though, that the Holy Spirit was working powerfully among them was not just through the miracles performed,[17] but, more importantly, through the powerful life transformation that happened in the lives of the Thessalonian believers. Paul cites how they "became an example to all the believers in Macedonia and in Achaia" (1 Thess. 1:7), how they "turned to God from idols to serve a living and true God" (1:9), and how they "endured the same sufferings at the hands of [their] own countrymen" (2:14) as the church in Jerusalem.

The Problem of the Modern Concept of Self

As exhilarating and life transforming as the proleptic blessings of the Holy Spirit are, they all hinge on the believer properly attending to this precious *arrabōn* of the future eighth-day blessings. But therein lies the problem for some. Somehow, the idea that someone's spirit should be in us in order to animate us is a concept hard to fathom. Our idea of the self does not seem to allow the indwelling of another spirit without sensing the violation of one's personhood. It is, thus, necessary to briefly address this issue if the gift of the indwelling Holy Spirit is to be properly understood and appropriated.

17. Based on Rom. 15:18–19, it is very likely that Paul is referring to miraculous deeds that accompany the proclamation of the gospel through the power of the Holy Spirit: "For I will not presume to speak of anything except what Christ has accomplished through me, resulting in the obedience of the Gentiles by word and deed, in the power of signs and wonders, in the power of the Spirit; so that from Jerusalem and round about as far as Illyricum I have fully preached the gospel of Christ." But, again, 1 Thess. 2:13 leaves the impression that the power of God is more than just miracles: "For this reason we also constantly thank God that when you received the word of God which you heard from us, you accepted it not as the word of men, but for what it really is, the word of God, which also performs its work in you who believe."

Grant Macaskill aptly points out that one of the possible obstacles to the proper appreciation of the indwelling Holy Spirit is our modern view of the self:

> As moderns, we are accustomed to speaking about a "person" or a "self" as if it were a thing in its own right, something that can be isolated from the world around it and still have a definable or describable identity. This is the concept that Charles Taylor famously labels the "buffered self."[18]

But such a way of thinking can be dangerous in that it misses the broader concept of an "I" or "self" that is formed in relational terms. "This is one of the reasons," Macaskill notes, "we find it difficult to comprehend what it means to say 'Christ lives in me' or 'to live is Christ': each of us assumes that we are an identity in our own right. We lack a category for our identity being formed through our relational encounter with another."[19]

But it is precisely this kind of relational notion of the self that the Bible would have us use to understand ourselves. To use Taylor's terminology, the biblical view of the self is not "buffered" but is "porous,"[20] whereby the influence of others can permeate and abide to the point of molding and shaping a life into the image of the influencer. Viewed this way, the indwelling Holy Spirit need not be feared as intrusive or coercive toward an existing self but rather embraced as complementing and enhancing such an entity.

Using an illustration borrowed from William Temple, John Stott helpfully explains the indwelling work of the Holy Spirit with this typical human limitation and the New Testament's proposed solution:

> It is no good giving me a play like Hamlet or King Lear, and telling me to write a play like that. Shakespeare could do it; I can't. And it is no good showing me a life like the life of Jesus and telling me to live a life like that. Jesus could do it; I can't. But if the genius of Shakespeare could come and live in me, then I could write plays like that. And if the Spirit of Jesus could come and live in me, then I could live a life like that. This is the secret of Christian sanctity. It is not that we should strive to live like Jesus, but that he by his Spirit should come and live in us.[21]

18. Macaskill, *Living in Union with Christ*, 5–6.
19. Macaskill, *Living in Union with Christ*, 6.
20. Taylor, *A Secular Age*, 37–41.
21. Stott, *Basic Christianity*, 102.

It is when we allow the life transforming influence of the Holy Spirit to flow into the deepest recess of our being that we experience the liberation that comes from the prolepsis of the eighth day of creation today. As we do, we cannot help but see what a gift the indwelling Holy Spirit of Christ is in us.

The Mechanics of the Infilling: Focusing on Our Love Relationship with Christ

Our discussion on the importance of the filling of the Holy Spirit naturally leads to the practical issue of its mechanics. There are different models of how the Holy Spirit is imparted to the believer. It is outside the purview of this book to explore all of them. But it will suffice for us to point out a key component that all the models have in common and that the Bible clearly teaches about the Spirit's filling.

The place to start is Jesus's own teaching concerning the Holy Spirit's purpose and function after Christ's ascension. Jesus says, "When the Helper comes, whom I will send to you from the Father, that is the Spirit of truth who proceeds from the Father, He will testify about Me" (John 15:26). And, again, in a more expansive description, he says, "But when He, the Spirit of truth, comes, He will guide you into all the truth; for He will not speak on His own initiative, but whatever He hears, He will speak; and He will disclose to you what is to come. He will glorify Me, for He will take of Mine and will disclose it to you" (John 16:13–14).

Note that in these two significant passages, Jesus shows us that the Holy Spirit is given not to glorify himself but Christ. The Holy Spirit did not usher in a new era centered on himself. There is a Christocentricity about his role and function in his indwelling work in the life of the believer.

With this theological understanding as our guide, we conclude that no matter what mode or model one may ascribe to the believer's infilling of the Holy Spirit, the Holy Spirit will always bring about a deepening of the believer's love relationship with Jesus Christ. The Holy Spirit will never seek to create a wedge between Jesus and the Holy Spirit in the interior life of the believer but rather, indeed, will even become voluntarily subservient to the glorification of Jesus Christ above himself. After all, the Holy Spirit is the Spirit of Christ (Rom. 8:9–10).[22] Therefore, in its simplest form, the filling of the Holy Spirit involves the believer focusing more of himself or herself on Jesus Christ. The deeper one's love for Christ becomes, the more the believer is said to be filled with the Spirit. As Stott puts it succinctly, "It is by the Spirit of Christ that we can be transformed into the image of Christ, *as we keep looking steadfastly towards him*."[23] This understanding is nicely depicted in Paul's prayer for the Ephesians, where he says,

> For this reason I bow my knees before the Father, from whom every family in heaven and on earth derives its name, that He would grant you, according to the riches of His glory, to be strengthened with power through His Spirit in the inner man, so that Christ may dwell in your hearts through faith; and that you, being rooted and grounded in love, may be able to comprehend with all the saints what is the breadth and length and height and depth, and to know the love of Christ which surpasses knowledge, that you may be filled up to all the fullness of God. (Eph. 3:14–19)

Thus, we have come full circle in this discussion of the filling of the Holy Spirit and have come back to the point made earlier that the indwelling Holy Spirit is accessed by a faith in Christ that has intensified and developed into love for Christ. We return to Paul's declaration in Galatians 2:20 that it was the love of Christ that motivated him to ultimately give of himself to Christ, which produced the phenomenon of living a life no longer for himself but for Christ and so intertwined with Christ that Paul could say that he has been crucified with Christ. It is this wondrous oneness with Christ as a result of the believer's faith grown into love for him that is the essence of the filling of the Holy Spirit. When oneness with Christ happens, we cannot help but experience proleptically aspects of the eighth day of creation in our time and in our lives.

22. In an interesting juxtaposition between the Holy Spirit and the Spirit of Christ, Paul clearly shows that these two terms are not only the same in essence but also complementary of each other in usage, thus demonstrating Christ's teaching that the Holy Spirit is his indwelling Spirit within the life of believers who has come to glorify Jesus Christ inside them. Paul writes, "However, you are not in the flesh but in the Spirit, if indeed the Spirit of God dwells in you. But if anyone does not have the Spirit of Christ, he does not belong to Him. If Christ is in you, though the body is dead because of sin, yet the spirit is alive because of righteousness" (Rom. 8:9–10).

23. Stott, *Basic Christianity*, 101 (emphasis added).

7

God's Providence in the "Already" of the Eighth Day of Creation, Part 2

Present Impact in Relation to the World

> If you become Christ's you will stumble upon wonder upon wonder, and every one of them true.
>
> —St. Brendan of Birr

Brendan was, of course, not exaggerating when he said those words about the effect that Christian conversion has on a person. Invariably, believers can attest to the veracity of his statement (even though they may vary in degree of experience). The reason the Christian life is an endless encounter of "wonder upon wonder" and every wonder true is that God has already inaugurated aspects of the future eighth day of creation for believers to inhabit today. As we have seen in the previous chapter, God has brought about the "already" components of the eighth day of creation through his "two hands": Jesus and the Holy Spirit. Five specific ways of experiencing that eighth-day wonder today were presented. The first two ways correspond directly to Jesus (through the incarnation of Christ) and the Holy Spirit (through the indwelling Holy

Spirit). They deal with the proleptic impact that the eighth day of creation has on our present relationship with the triune God.

In this chapter, the last three ways will be discussed. They are by nature an extension of the incarnation of Christ (Christology) and the indwelling of the Holy Spirit (pneumatology). And they deal with the proleptic impact that the eighth day of creation has on our present relationship with the world at large. Thus, we continue now with the believer's personal narrative in Christ, the communion of saints, and the synchronizing to God's time.

Five Ways for Appropriating Proleptically God's Eighth Day of Creation (Nos. 3–5)

3. Through the Believer's Personal Narrative in Christ

The eighth day of creation can be experienced proleptically through the adoption of a new personal history or narrative. It stands to reason that this should be so. If, as we noted earlier, our self-perception is bound up in Christ through the work of the Holy Spirit in us, then whatever our previous identity was must necessarily be enveloped by the narrative of the One to whom we are deeply related and to whom we owe our ultimate allegiance. This forms our new mental model of self. It is based on this new story we live in that we experience the new reality we are presently inhabiting. For the Christian, that new reality involves aspects of the eighth day of creation. It is imperative that Christians know and enter into this new narrative that we have been given through Christ if we are to truly experience its blessings today.

A powerful example of the importance of a personal narrative is found in an Old Testament requirement during the observance of the Feast of Weeks (Pentecost), which is related in Deuteronomy 26. As the worshipers offer up their firstfruits sacrifice to the priest during the feast, they are required to recite a narrative account to the priest as part of their spiritual act of worship before God. Beginning in verse 5, it retells the story of how Jacob and his family prospered in their difficult sojourn in Egypt. "My father was a wandering Aramean, and he went down to Egypt and sojourned there, few in number; but there he became a great, mighty and populous nation." But then the subsequent verses shift the point of view from the ancestors of the past to incorporate the worshipers in the present. In a not-so-subtle yet sublime way, the recitation of the narrative suddenly incorporates the present-day worshipers into the story:

> And the Egyptians treated *us* harshly and afflicted *us*, and imposed hard labor on *us*. Then *we* cried to the LORD, the God of our fathers, and the LORD heard *our* voice and saw *our* affliction and *our* toil and *our* oppression; and the LORD brought *us* out of Egypt with a mighty hand and an outstretched arm and with great terror and with signs and wonders; and He has brought *us* to this place and has given *us* this land, a land flowing with milk and honey. (vv. 6–9 [emphasis added])

It is only after entering into the narrative in a personalized way that the worshipers are permitted to offer up their sacrifice and utter these words: "Now behold, I have brought the first of the produce of the ground which You, O LORD have given me" (v. 10). Such an internalizing and personalizing of the narrative makes sense in light of what God would further require of them: "And you shall set it [the offering] down before the LORD your God, and worship before the LORD your God; and you and the Levite and the alien who is among you shall rejoice in all the good which the LORD your God has given you and your household" (vv. 10–11). The recitation enabled the worshipers not only to enter the narrative but also to own it and live it out by now generously sharing the bounty of their harvest with the Lord, the Levites, and the aliens in a spirit of sincere and spontaneous rejoicing, supplied and stimulated by the personal narrative prescribed in Deuteronomy.

The Old Testament practice cited above while ancient is certainly supported by Alasdair MacIntyre's famous dictum: "I can only answer the question 'What am I to do?' if I can answer the prior question 'Of what story or stories do I find myself a part?'"[1] So how does a person today, living in the New Testament era, embrace and enter into such a new narrative so as to not only transform one's life but also access proleptically the future eighth day of creation? The following are some ways to do so.

One very obvious way that the apostle Peter points us to is found in his first epistle. There he encourages the early church in Asia Minor, made up mostly of gentile believers, to take on the narrative of the people of God:

1. MacIntyre, *After Virtue*, 216.

> But you are a chosen race, a royal priesthood, a holy nation, a people for God's own possession, so that you may proclaim the excellencies of Him who has called you out of darkness into His marvelous light; for you once were not a people, but now you are the people of God; you had not received mercy, but now you have received mercy. (1 Pet. 2:9–10)

Certainly, this counsel makes good sense because believers, indeed, are the people of God. As such, there is a sense in which gentile believers are entitled to partake of the promises that God made to Israel in the Old Testament concerning the coming new covenant (Jer. 31). On that basis, gentile believers could claim to also be the people of God today through Jesus Christ.[2] But, admittedly, this approach may be difficult for some to take because it raises the hermeneutical and theological issue of replacement theology—that is, the debate on whether the church replaced Israel as the people of God. It is outside the purview of this work to delve into that complicated discussion. It is enough, however, to say that there are other ways to establish a personal narrative in Christ without being stranded in the quagmire of that debate.

Another approach that can be taken from the Bible is through a familial model found at the heart of the gospel message. The New Testament states that believers are adopted as children of God through Jesus Christ (Rom. 8:15–17; Gal. 4:4–7). In this way of seeing ourselves, Jesus is even understood as our older brother (Heb. 2:11–12). Using this metaphor, believers are invited to follow through the underlying narrative arc of the metaphor. As God's adopted children, we will one day, in the eschaton, inherit what the Father wants to bestow on us through his Son (Rom. 8:18–23; 1 Pet. 1:3–9). Moreover, as a proud Father, he will ensure that his adopted children will become his own glorious inheritances (Eph. 1:11, 18). The more we see ourselves in light of this new narrative of ourselves in Christ and live in its reality, the more we begin to taste proleptically the future eighth day of creation blessing in our present world. The reason is that we will begin to behave in a manner consistent with our self-narrative and who we will eventually become one day.

In an excellent treatment of the topic of the believer's sonship, J. I. Packer makes the bold declaration that "*the entire Christian life has to*

2. Some would even argue that this is what Paul intended to say when he described the Galatian believers, mostly gentiles, to be "the Israel of God" (Gal. 6:16).

be understood in terms of it. Sonship must be the controlling thought—normative category, if you like—at every point."[3] Packer explains, "Now, just as the knowledge of His unique sonship controlled Jesus's living of His own life on earth, so He insists that the knowledge of our adoptive sonship must control our lives too."[4] In fact, Packer goes so far as to say,

> If you want to judge how well a person understands Christianity, find out how much he makes of the thought of being God's child, and having God as his Father. If this is not the thought that prompts his worship and prayers and his whole outlook on life, it means that he does not understand Christianity very well at all.[5]

This bold assertion is biblically supported. For as Paul said, one of the things that the Holy Spirit does is lead us into this sonship narrative when we become believers in Christ. Twice in Scripture Paul does this, underlining its importance to our self-understanding:

> For you have not received a spirit of slavery leading to fear again, but you have received a spirit of adoption as sons by which we cry out, "Abba! Father!" The Spirit Himself testifies with our spirit that we are children of God, and if children, heirs also, heirs of God and fellow heirs with Christ, if indeed we suffer with Him so that we may also be glorified with Him. (Rom. 8:15–17)

> But when the fullness of the time came, God sent forth His Son, born of a woman, born under the Law, so that He might redeem those who were under the Law, that we might receive the adoption as sons. Because you are sons, God has sent forth the Spirit of His Son into our hearts, crying, "Abba! Father!" Therefore you are no longer a slave, but a son; and if a son, then an heir through God. (Gal. 4:4–7)

No doubt entering into this narrative can be, at times, hard to do, especially in our day and age when different narratives are being paraded for us to choose from as if in a marketplace. It is, therefore, hard to know if the narrative that we embrace is genuine or make-believe. But this is why Paul

3. Packer, *Knowing God*, 190.
4. Packer, *Knowing God*, 190.
5. Packer, *Knowing God*, 182.

interceded for the believers in the region of Ephesus this way: "I pray that the eyes of your heart may be enlightened, so that you will know what is the hope of His calling, what are the riches of the glory of His inheritance in the saints, and what is the surpassing greatness of His power toward us who believe" (Eph. 1:18–19). This prayer for a proper self-narrative is one in which we should also pray for ourselves and for fellow believers. For often believers do not really know the narrative of their sonship and, therefore, fail to enter into the proleptic experience of the eighth day of creation, when believers in Christ will, in fact, be revealed in the eschaton as children of God (Rom. 8:18–23; 1 John 3:1–2).

Packer gently challenges each believer with these soul-searching questions: "Do I, as a Christian, understand myself? Do I know my own real identity? My own real destiny?"[6] In case we are unsure of how to answer these questions affirmatively, Packer proceeds to suggest the following:

> *I am a child of God. God is my Father; heaven is my home; every day is one day nearer. My Saviour is my brother; every Christian is my brother too.* Say it over and over to yourself first thing in the morning, last thing at night, as you wait for the bus, any time your mind is free, and ask that you may be enabled to live as one who knows it is all utterly and completely true.[7]

Packer's exact wording for us to recite meditatively and prayerfully may not have the elegance of Deuteronomy 26:5–9, but it works to instill in us the narrative we must have if we are to experience proleptically what the eighth day of creation will one day reveal us to be. For as he says so eloquently, "This is the Christian's secret of a *Christian* life, and of a *God-honouring* life: and these are the aspects of the situation that really matter. May the secret become fully yours, and fully mine."[8]

4. *Through the Communion of the Saints (the Church)*

George Ladd correctly observes that the church is not the kingdom of God (the full manifestation of the promised eighth day of creation). Rather, "the Kingdom is the rule of God; the church is a society of men."[9]

6. Packer, *Knowing God*, 207.
7. Packer, *Knowing God*, 207
8. Packer, *Knowing God*, 208.
9. Ladd, *Presence of the Future*, 262.

But Ladd also insightfully points out that there is a close relationship between the two. "There can be no Kingdom without a church. . . . And there can be no church without God's Kingdom."[10] For the church is the custodian of the kingdom who holds the "key" to the kingdom.[11] Anyone who desires to experience proleptically the blessings of the eighth day of creation must necessarily involve the church as God has designed it to be. Ladd explains,

> Before Pentecost, the life and blessings of the Kingdom of God were experienced in fellowship with the person of the historical Jesus. After Pentecost, they were experienced by the indwelling Christ through the Spirit. Both of these are blessings of the age to come. We have seen that among the blessings of the Kingdom in Jesus' ministry were forgiveness and fellowship, especially table fellowship with Jesus . . . After Pentecost, this table fellowship was continued, but in a new form. Believers everywhere assemble at table with one another (Acts 2:46; 1 Cor. 11:20ff.) invoking the presence of Christ in the Spirit. The Aramaic prayer *marana tha* in 1 Corinthians 16:22 is probably a prayer not only for the Parousia of Christ but also for his visitation of the church and Christian fellowship (*Didache* 10:6).[12]

In short, then, to use the language of the Apostles' Creed, it is in the midst of "the communion of the saints" that the Holy Spirit enables us to experience proleptically today all the blessings of the eighth day of creation accomplished in Christ.

That the church should be God's conduit makes perfect sense in light of the Holy Spirit's relationship to believers. Since the Spirit indwells them, the corporate assembly of believers renders the gathering as tantamount to a temple reminiscent of the one in Jerusalem, except that this one is mobile and dynamic. Jesus said in Matthew 18:20, "For where two or three have gathered together in My name, I am there in their midst." Moreover, Paul made the temple imagery even more explicit in 1 Corinthians 3:16–17: "Do you not know that you are a temple of God and that the Spirit of God dwells in you? If any man destroys the temple of God, God will destroy him, for the temple of God is holy, and that is what

10. Ladd, *Presence of the Future*, 277.
11. Ladd, *Presence of the Future*, 273–77.
12. Ladd, *Presence of the Future*, 273.

you are." Succinctly, in 2 Corinthians 6:16, Paul simply says, "We are the temple of the living God."

So how then does the church channel proleptically the eighth day of creation for our benefit? The following are four ways God has manifested his providence through the church in our world today:

- the church in worship
- the church in mutual nurture
- the church in exercise of responsible authority
- the church in transposition

These are not exhaustive, but they are representative of how the church serves as a conduit for the proleptic experience of the eighth day of creation.

The Church in Worship

As mentioned in chapter 4, one of the things that characterizes the eighth day of creation is the ceaseless worship of God with all the saints in heaven. The church provides this same experience as the saints on earth mirror this eternal activity now. And when the saints worship God today, something happens to them. In the poetic words of Charles Wesley, we become "lost in wonder, love, and praise."[13]

Psalm 22:3 says, "You are holy, O You who are enthroned upon the praises of Israel." This verse could be understood as referring to the subjective experience of God as enthroned or inhabiting the praises of his people. Or it could be a reference of a more objective experience of acknowledging that God is enthroned or inhabits his people whenever he is worshiped by his people. The former understanding seems preferrable. But in either case, there is a centering of the believer's life around the being of God that reflects how things should be. He is our God, and we are the people of his pasture.

When we worship, we experience how our existence is supposed to be. Worship enables us to enter into that future hope and grasp it in our hearts momentarily as long as we are in that state of worship. Such a proleptic experience, however, will not remain as a sentiment but will naturally, in

13. Charles Wesley, "Love Divine, All Loves Excelling," hymn, 1747.

time, translate itself into a consistent action, reflecting in us the glimpse and foretaste of that glorious eighth day of creation.

The Church in Mutual Nurture

In one of his sermons Augustine observed how similar yet different are the faith developments of Jesus's first disciples and his subsequent disciples. He said, "Their faith has been fulfilled, and so has ours; theirs fulfilled from seeing the head [the risen Christ], ours from seeing the body [the church throughout all the nations]."[14]

Augustine's statement is more profound than he could ever have imagined because it is both biblical and existentially relevant today. We do not physically see the risen Jesus Christ today. But we can see his body—the church—that he redeemed. By looking at it and participating in it, we can develop our faith. Thus, Paul would heartily confirm the truthfulness of what Augustine declared. Writing to the Ephesians, Paul describes the church as the body of Christ, which is being built up by the Spirit through the spiritual gifts he gives to each believer.

> As a result, we are no longer to be children, tossed here and there by waves and carried about by every wind of doctrine, by the trickery of men, by craftiness in deceitful scheming; but speaking the truth in love, we are to grow up in all aspects into Him who is the head, even Christ, from whom the whole body, being fitted and held together by what every joint supplies, according to the proper working of each individual part, causes the growth of the body for the building up of itself in love. (Eph. 4:14–16)

This work of transformation in human souls that unites them to Christ their head is the ultimate telos of the eighth day of creation. By bringing about this end progressively in the life of the believer today, the church shows itself truly to be a conduit for God's prolepsis of that glorious future he has in store for us. The church's work, however, not only is a work of future anticipation but also is a present liberation from the power of sin through the power of Christ's Holy Spirit, who resides within the communion of the saints.

When the church is engaged in mutual nurture through the exercise of their spiritual gifts, this is nothing less than showing the *agapē* love that

14. Augustine, "Sermon 116," in *Sermons 94A–147A*, 206.

Jesus commanded of his disciples in John 13:34. The result is that faith is developed and all will come to know that this gathering is the assembly of Christ's disciples. It represents the present embodiment (prolepsis) of the future eighth day of creation.

The Church in Exercise of Responsible Authority

If the church is to be a community in prolepsis of the eighth day of creation, then one of the things that it should mirror in miniature is the reign of Christ within the community of faith. Jesus Christ will one day reign on earth, not alone but together with the saints. The church is an outpost of the coming kingdom, and it is clear that Jesus Christ has given his community of followers authority on earth to some extent in anticipation of the full coming reign. This authority is given not to stoke our pride or elevate our self-esteem but rather for the benefit of the spiritually lost humanity that needs to be rescued as we have been rescued also by Christ.

In Matthew 16:18–20, upon Peter's declaration that Jesus is the Christ, the Son of the living God, Jesus gives Peter the "keys of the kingdom of heaven," and to him Christ further says, "Whatever you bind on earth shall have been bound in heaven, and whatever you loose on earth shall have been loosed in heaven" (v. 19). At first glance, it seems like Peter has been given carte blanche to do anything he wants with whomever he wants, and that this privilege was given to him alone. But upon closer examination, we see that the keys or the power to bind and loose has to do with the truth of Peter's declaration about Jesus. To the extent that he proclaims the same declaration that he made about Jesus Christ, Peter is properly exercising kingdom authority that will lead to a soul's entry into the kingdom of God.

In case the foregoing interpretation is disputed, we note that in the Gospel of John, Jesus makes a same similar statement but makes it more obvious that forgiveness of sin is the object and that the authority is not confined to a few but to all disciples: "Jesus said to them again, 'Peace be with you; as the Father has sent Me, I also send you.' And when He had said this, He breathed on them and said to them, 'Receive the Holy Spirit. If you forgive the sins of any, their sins have been forgiven them; if you retain the sins of any, they have been retained'" (John 20:21–23). Thus, even now believers reign with Christ in the act of fulfilling the Great Commission.

Every time a believer evangelizes, and especially when believers do so corporately as the church, the eighth day of creation reign with Christ is experienced proleptically. In many ways, this ought to cause believers to want to experience more of this reigning with Christ in this lifetime by such loving and responsible means.

The proleptic eschatological authority that Christ conferred on the church is not to be applied just to those outside the church in the form of missions or evangelism. Indeed, this authority also covers those within the church. Two very graphic examples in the New Testament of the church having been given such authority are seen in the area of church discipline and the adjudication of disputes within the community of faith.

Jesus himself says that in a case where a sinning believer refuses to repent, the church is to exercise discipline on such a one, provided the procedure that he lays out has been properly followed (Matt. 18:15–20). As a last resort, Jesus says, "If he refuses to listen to them [two or three witnesses], tell it to the church; and if he refuses to listen even to the church, let him be to you as a Gentile and a tax collector. Truly I say to you, whatever you bind on earth shall have been bound in heaven; and whatever you loose on earth shall have been loosed in heaven" (vv. 17–18). Note the same binding and loosing language is used to denote authority.

The early church certainly was not shy in exercising such an authority. In 1 Corinthians 5:1–5, Paul is very explicit in telling the Corinthian church to discipline a person who was having an affair with his father's wife (most likely his stepmother). This was done for the sake of upholding God's moral standard and for the sake of purifying the church (vv. 9–13). But it should be noted that the goal of such disciplinary action is not punitive per se but rehabilitative. If 2 Corinthians 2:6–11 is a reference to the same incident that Paul addressed in 1 Corinthians 5, then in what follows, Paul is telling the Corinthian church to cease the discipline, since the person has already repented:

> Sufficient for such a one is this punishment which was inflicted by the majority, so that on the contrary you should rather forgive and comfort him, otherwise such a one might be overwhelmed by excessive sorrow. Wherefore I urge you to reaffirm your love for him. For to this end also I wrote, so that I might put you to the test, whether you are obedient in all things. But one whom you forgive anything, I forgive also; for indeed what I have

> forgiven, if I have forgiven anything, I did it for your sakes in the presence of Christ, so that no advantage would be taken of us by Satan, for we are not ignorant of his schemes.

Regardless of whether 2 Corinthians 2:6–11 deals with the same person mentioned in 1 Corinthians 5, there is ample evidence from the teachings of Jesus and the practices of the early church to support the general principle that loving rehabilitation, not harsh retribution, is the goal of the Christian community's exercise of its authority.

Aside from the situation of a sinning believer, the early church has also exercised authority when adjudicating disputes among believers. Indeed, Paul says in 1 Corinthians 6:1–6 that it is the only recourse believers should use, and they should not turn to law courts outside the church. In response to believers in the church in Corinth suing one another, the apostle Paul chides them, "Does any one of you, when he has a case against his neighbor, dare to go to law before the unrighteous and not before the saints?" (1 Cor. 6:1).

The reason that Paul gives for why believers are to turn to the church for arbitration is most interesting and reflects the practical use of the prolepsis of the eighth day of creation. He says,

> Do you not know that the saints will judge the world? If the world is judged by you, are you not competent to constitute the smallest law courts? Do you not know that we will judge angels? How much more matters of this life? So if you have law courts dealing with matters of this life, do you appoint them as judges who are of no account in the church? I say this to your shame. Is it so, that there is not among you one wise man who will be able to decide between his brethren, but brother goes to law with brother, and that before unbelievers? (1 Cor. 6:1–6)

Moreover, Paul does not lose sight of the motive of love and the well-being of fellow believers as the goal of the Christian community. He adds, "Actually, then, it is already a defeat for you, that you have lawsuits with one another. Why not rather be wronged? Why not rather be defrauded? On the contrary, you yourselves wrong and defraud. You do this even to your brethren" (1 Cor. 6:7–8).

Thus, to be a Christian is to be a part of the communion of saints, who not only are looking forward to the eighth day of creation but also are even now beginning to live out its reality within the community of Christ's followers in a responsible way. The early church has demonstrated that well for us. And it is something that present-day believers must also take seriously.

The Church in Transposition

Two characteristics of the eighth day of creation are that the saints will see God (Rev. 22:4; cf. 21:3) and that they will reign with Christ (Rev. 22:5). Are these events accessible for us today? They seem so remote and so far from our present reality. Yet they are, in fact, part of the prolepsis of the eighth day of creation open to us today as believers in Christ through the communion of the saints.

In John Calvin's treatment of the Lord's Supper in *Institutes of the Christian Religion*, he deals with the thorny issue of in what sense is the bread and wine in the Lord's Supper the body and the blood of Christ. Immediately, Calvin makes the obvious claim that the physical entity of Christ is in heaven by virtue of his ascension. Thus, whatever is meant by the bread being the body of Christ and the wine being the blood of Christ can only be symbolic in nature. Yet it is a powerful symbolism that leads the worshiper into a real encounter with the glorified Christ by faith through the work of the Holy Spirit. The Holy Spirit is "the bond" and the "channel through which all that Christ himself is and has is conveyed to us."[15]

So far, Calvin is only saying what other theologians have said. What is unique in his approach is saying that instead of bringing Christ down to us during the observance of the Lord's Supper for that moment in communion, the Holy Spirit actually brings us to Christ—a kind of transposition as we properly observe the Lord's Supper. Marveling at this approach, historian Justo González comments,

> In most textbooks—including my own—Calvin's understanding of communion is discussed in terms of how Christ is present in it. Posing the question in this manner, a spectrum of Protestant views is commonly drawn, with Luther at one end, Zwingli at another, and Calvin someplace in between. While there is a measure of truth in this, it tends to obscure Calvin's

15. Calvin, *Institutes* 4.17.12 (2:1373).

> particular perspective on the matter. Luther, Roman Catholics, and Zwingli debated how Christ comes to be present at communion. Calvin deals with this question in a different way. For him it is not so much a matter of Christ coming to us in communion, as it is of our being taken to his presence in a proleptic prefiguration of the heavenly banquet. Since this takes place by virtue of the Holy Spirit, Calvin's view is often called "virtualism."[16]

In the following passage from the *Institutes*, Calvin makes his view explicit:

> 31. Christ not brought down to us; we are lifted up to him
>
> But greatly mistaken are those who conceive no presence of flesh in the Supper unless it lies in the bread. For thus they leave nothing to the secret working of the Spirit, which unites Christ himself to us. To them Christ does not seem present unless he comes down to us. As though, if he should lift us to himself, we should not just as much enjoy his presence! The question is therefore only of the manner, for they place Christ in the bread, while we do not think it lawful for us to drag him from heaven. Let our readers decide which one is more correct. Only away with that calumny that Christ is removed from his Supper unless he lies hidden under the covering of bread! For since this mystery is heavenly, there is no need to draw Christ to earth that he may be joined to us.[17]

How the Holy Spirit transposes us to the very presence of Christ in heaven is "the secret working of the Spirit" or a "mystery."[18] But Calvin

16. González, "John Calvin," 120. González speculates, "Calvin is very much engaged with the congregation in Geneva, but Geneva is not his home. In a sense, France is his home but the France for which he yearns does not actually exist, and in the actual France he probably would be even less at home than he is in Geneva. So, to him it is not enough to say that Christ comes to the gathered congregation in Geneva. Christ certainly does that. But what is most important is that, by the power or virtue of the Holy Spirit, the Genevan congregation is taken up to heaven, to eat with congregations in France, and in Germany, and elsewhere. And following Calvin in his understanding of communion, it is clear to see that this yearning to be with the heavenly host—in union with Christ, reflects the yearning of the exiles. Exiles know that they are not at home in any earthly city, and for this reason, they are the ones who are able to capture, in their own reality, the meaning of communion. Furthermore, they can teach us not only about the importance of communion but also about the Christian life as well as theological methodology. A methodology, where being an exile is not a deficit, but rather this condition, gives us a glimpse to God's reign, the presence of Christ in our lives, and provides a new look to the Protestant Reformation. May God help us to see and experience Christ in those who are in exile, and may we learn from them and their example" (120).

17. Calvin, *Institutes* 4.17.31 (2:1403).

18. Calvin, *Institutes* 4.17.31 (2:1403).

is clear that "we are lifted up to heaven with our eyes and minds, to seek Christ there in the glory of his Kingdom."[19] In short, it involves our proper understanding and imagination of the bread and the wine as "the symbols [that] invite us to him in his wholeness."[20] There, in that state of being lifted to the very presence of Christ in heaven, our souls are fed with the transcendent reality that "he shows his presence in power and strength, is always among his own people, and breathes his life upon them, and lives in them, sustaining them, strengthening, quickening, keeping them unharmed, as if he were present in the body."[21] Indeed, we come to understand that, even though Jesus Christ has been "received into heaven in your very sight, he has claimed his heavenly empire; it remains for you patiently to wait until he comes again as judge of the world. For he has now entered heaven, not to possess it by himself, but to gather you and all godly people with him."[22] The ascension calls us not only to experience an aspect of the future to come but also to participate in that future reign now within our own humble circumstances in life. This transposition during the Lord's Supper through the Holy Spirit then becomes a prolepsis of the eighth day of creation with the present benefit of emboldening us to live our lives for Christ in the last days of the seventh day faithfully.

At first glance, what Calvin depicts seems spectacular and speculative without scriptural warrant. But, upon closer examination, everything he says is grounded in the Pauline teaching found in the New Testament. In Ephesians, Paul says that, as part of Christ's redemptive work in the life of the believer, God has already "raised us up with Him, and seated us with Him in the heavenly places in Christ Jesus" (2:6). The "with Him" reference is a clear indication that Paul had in mind a prolepsis of the believer in the future reign of Christ today. To further underscore this point, Paul indicates that God the Father has "seated Him at His right hand in the heavenly places, far above all rule and authority and power and dominion, and every name that is named, not only in this age but also in the one to come" (1:20–21). But for what purpose and for whose benefit? Paul makes it explicit: "He put all things in subjection under His

19. Calvin, *Institutes* 4.17.18 (2:1381).
20. Calvin, *Institutes* 4.17.18 (2:1381).
21. Calvin, *Institutes* 4.17.18 (2:1381).
22. Calvin, *Institutes* 4.17.27 (2:1395).

feet, and gave Him as head over all things to the church, which is His body, the fullness of Him who fills all in all" (1:22–23). It is so that the church—even now—might benefit from the resurrected and ascended position of Jesus Christ, who is presently seated at the right hand of the Father.[23] In this sense, Calvin is not stating anything novel but merely repeating Paul in his discussion of the Spirit elevating believers to the presence of Christ so that they might "seek Christ there in the glory of his Kingdom"[24] for their living today.

The only difference is that Calvin uses the Lord's Supper as the means for accessing this transposition of the Spirit, whereas Paul uses his apostolic prayer in Ephesians 1:18–19, where he asks of God the Father that "the eyes of your heart may be enlightened, so that you will know what is the hope of His calling, what are the riches of the glory of His inheritance in the saints, and what is the surpassing greatness of His power toward us who believe." In both instances the underlying concern is the same. God has given so many future blessings in Christ to believers that we have not yet fully tapped into in their present existence. The key once again, however, is what both Paul and Calvin have demonstrated for us: the two hands of God—Jesus Christ and the Holy Spirit.

5. *Through Synchronizing to God's Time*

Another characteristic of the eighth day of creation depicted in the Bible is that there is another way of reckoning or measuring each passing moment in that future existence. According to John, in the new heaven and the new earth, the new Jerusalem will come down from God to earth in order become the dwelling of the saints. But, interestingly, John says,

> And the city has no need of the sun or of the moon to shine on it, for the glory of God has illumined it, and its lamp is the Lamb. The nations will

23. Theologians debate whether this "seated at the right hand of God" constitutes his present reigning or a future one. It is outside the purview of this present work to get into this debate. It is enough, however, to say that there is an "already and not yet" phenomenon at work here. To be sure, the reign of Christ is fully manifested in the future. But this passage and others seem to indicate that Christ, who is the second member of the Trinity and exalted by the Father, presently holds authority in this present era to be of assistance to his church. It is this power derived from his resurrected and ascended exalted position that is the beginning of the eighth day of creation that he now shares with believers today.

24. Calvin, *Institutes* 4.17.18 (2:1381).

> walk by its light, and the kings of the earth will bring their glory into it. In the daytime (for there will be no night there) its gates will never be closed. (Rev. 21:23–25)

This observation is confirmed by the prophet Zechariah's own vision of that day:

> In that day there will be no light; the luminaries will dwindle. For it will be a unique day which is known to the LORD, neither day nor night, but it will come about that at evening time there will be light. (Zech. 14:6–7)

In the new creation, then, time will not be as we know it. The sun (or any other heavenly body) will not be the measure of time, but the Son himself.

What a glorious event that will be when every moment of our existence centers on the triune God! But is such a future event accessible to us today so as to benefit us? The answer is yes. From its inception till now, the church has sought to synchronize its time to that future time of God. This is seen especially in the corporate worship of the church. The church is a community that has begun to live in God's eternal time because of the revelation it has received concerning the eighth day of creation.

The Bible recognizes the idea of *chronos* time—the chronological passage of time. But it also recognizes the concept of *kairos* time—the arrival of a divine occasion or opportunity, the right season for God's purposes. While every living creature lives through *chronos* time, not everyone lives in *kairos* time, since not everyone recognizes such a momentous occasion so as to live in light of it. The coming of Jesus Christ into the world is the most important *kairos* moment, which, if received and responded to properly, ushers us into a new way of reckoning our earthly existence. This existence is no longer based on a life revolving around the sun or some other earthly way of measuring life; it is centered in Jesus Christ and his work on our behalf. This is why when Jesus started his ministry, he proclaimed, "The time [*kairos*] is fulfilled, and the kingdom of God is at hand; repent and believe in the gospel" (Mark 1:15). This declaration is not an empty one but rather is supported by the manifestations of the coming kingdom of God at the center of the eighth-day creation. When emissaries from John the Baptist ask Jesus if he really is the Messiah, who is to usher in this new day and time, Jesus sends word to him:

> Go and report to John what you have seen and heard: the blind receive sight, the lame walk, the lepers are cleansed, and the deaf hear, the dead are raised up, the poor have the gospel preached to them. Blessed is he who does not take offense at Me. (Luke 7:22–23)

Unlike John the Baptist, the church eventually understood that Christ's full manifestation of the eighth day of creation will not happen until his second advent. But that does not diminish their understanding of the *kairos* time they live in. In fact, it accentuates the fact that they live in the last moments of the seventh day and the beginning of the eighth day of creation. D. A. Carson makes this helpful comment about the New Testament church's awareness of the time they live in:

> Commonly when the Bible speaks about the "last days," it refers to the entire period between Christ's first coming and his second. . . . The idea is that the coming of Christ is so world transforming, now that the Kingdom has already dawned, that the old world is petering out; it is coming to an end. We are now, already, in the last days.[25]

In light of this awareness, the New Testament is replete with exhortations to believers that use this new sense of time (that they are in the last days) to live their lives responsibly and to organize their lives accordingly. Paul's teaching in Romans 13:11–13 is paradigmatic:

> Do this, knowing the time, that it is already the hour for you to awaken from sleep; for now salvation is nearer to us than when we believed. The night is almost gone, and the day is near. Therefore let us lay aside the deeds of darkness and put on the armor of light. Let us behave properly as in the day, not in carousing and drunkenness, not in sexual promiscuity and sensuality, not in strife and jealousy.

Specifically, when believers are facing hardships and even injustice, the apostle James gives the command: "You too be patient; strengthen your hearts, for the coming of the Lord is near" (James 5:8). Note Peter's exhortation to pray: "The end of all things is near; therefore, be of sound judgment and sober spirit for the purpose of prayer" (1 Pet. 4:7). Consistently

25. Carson, *From the Resurrection to His Return*, 11–12.

assembling together finds its rationale in the eschaton: "not forsaking our own assembling together, as is the habit of some, but encouraging one another; and all the more as you see the day drawing near" (Heb. 10:25). Reading and obeying Scripture also draws importance from the imminent return of Christ: "Blessed is he who reads and those who hear the words of the prophecy, and heed the things which are written in it; for the time is near" (Rev. 1:3).

More startlingly, Paul uses the fact that believers are living in the dawn of the eighth day as the basis for making decisions on many mundane (but important) issues. In 1 Corinthians 7, Paul prefaces his advice to believers this way:

> But this I say, brethren, the time has been shortened, so that from now on those who have wives should be as though they had none; and those who weep, as though they did not weep; and those who rejoice, as though they did not rejoice; and those who buy, as though they did not possess; and those who use the world, as though they did not make full use of it; for the form of this world is passing away. (7:29–31)

Then, with consistent application of the principle stated above, he tells the widows in the church this:

> But I want you to be free from concern. One who is unmarried is concerned about the things of the Lord, how he may please the Lord; but one who is married is concerned about the things of the world, how he may please his wife, and his interests are divided. The woman who is unmarried, and the virgin, is concerned about the things of the Lord, that she may be holy both in body and spirit; but one who is married is concerned about the things of the world, how she may please her husband. This I say for your own benefit; not to put a restraint upon you, but to promote what is appropriate and to secure undistracted devotion to the Lord. (7:32–35)

With the same controlling principle of the coming eschaton in view, Paul counsels slaves who might become stressed about their inability to get their freedom:

> Were you called while a slave? Do not worry about it; but if you are able also to become free, rather do that. For he who was called in the Lord while a slave,

> is the Lord's freedman; likewise he who was called while free, is Christ's slave. You were bought with a price; do not become slaves of men. Brethren, each one is to remain with God in that condition in which he was called. (7:21–24)

Paul portrays a Christian life that is subsumed under the reality of the imminent return of Christ. When done this way, it is easy to see how the proleptic effect of the eighth day of creation can definitely be experienced by believers living during this time.[26]

To help steer us into these life decisions that are Christ-centered and focused on the eighth day of creation, the New Testament church since its inception has helpfully instilled in its members a different "internal" time or clock that reflects this new *kairos* time that the church lives in. The church restructured the community of faith's rhythm of life to Sunday. The day of worship for the Christian community revolves around Sunday[27]—the Lord's Day, the day that Jesus rose from the dead and, thus, ushers in the dawning of the eighth day of creation. The move may seem insignificant from the outside, but it is very transformative internally for the lives of believers. When done properly, it enables them to live proleptically on the eighth day of creation. For it serves as a deliberate weekly reminder for the believer to live anachronistically with *chronos* time and to live proleptically in light of the dawning of the eighth day of creation. While everyone else might center their rhythm of life on other days or other factors, believers who center their rhythm of life on the Lord's Day cannot help but enter into it anew every week. And that experience helps to reinforce not only

26. This emphasis on the eschatological eighth day of creation, however, does not mean that Christians are to mindlessly or passively accept the status quo, especially when moral wrongs are at issue. In this passage, 1 Cor. 7, we see Paul beautifully balancing the eschatological emphasis with the opportunities or needs that one encounters in life. So, to slaves Paul could say, "Were you called while a slave? Do not worry about it; but if you are able also to become free, rather do that" (v. 21). Or he could counsel singles and widows, "But I say to the unmarried and to widows that it is good for them if they remain even as I. But if they do not have self-control, let them marry; for it is better to marry than to burn with passion" (vv. 8–9). How this balancing is to be done in a specific situation, obviously, would require much seeking of the Lord's wisdom and guidance in prayer. But Paul's main point is that the eschatological eighth day of creation should be the reigning paradigm for how believers live today.

27. For the most part, Saturday still remained as the Sabbath day of rest that some Christians, especially Jewish Christians, observed. But Sunday—despite the fact that it was a working day, being the first day of the week—was the day when believers congregated very early to worship before going to work. And, again, at the end of their work day they would congregate in the evening to worship as a community centered on Christ, who rose from the dead.

the unique *kairos* time we live in but also the decisions and lifestyles drawn from the eighth day of creation that we must live out.

Theologian Alexander Schmemann makes an astute observation about the problems that believers have today and the need to return to proper worship that centers on the Lord's Day:

> We must return from this to the fundamental Christian dichotomy, which is between the old and the new. 'Behold, I make all things new' (Rev. 21:5). Notice that Christ does not say 'I create new things,' but 'all things new.' Such is the eschatological vision that should mark our eucharistic celebration on each Lord's Day.
>
> Nowadays we treat the Day of the Lord as the seventh day, the Sabbath. For the Fathers it was the eighth day, the first day of the new creation, the day on which the Church not only remembers the past but also remembers, indeed enters into, the future, the last and great day.[28]

But why is the observance of this day so important? Schmemann says it is because of what happens to us when we worship with a view toward the eighth day of creation that Christ provided for us:

> It is the day on which the Church assembles, locking the doors, and ascends to the point at which it becomes possible to say, "Holy, holy, holy Lord God of Sabaoth, heaven and earth are full of thy glory." Tell me, what right do we have to say that?
>
> Today I read the *London Times*—a welcome change from the *New York Times*—but, whichever of them we read, does it make us say, "Heaven and earth are full of thy glory"? The world which they show us is certainly not full of the glory of God.
>
> If we make such an affirmation in the Liturgy, it is not just an expression of Christian optimism ("Onward, Christian soldiers"), but simply and solely because we have ascended to the point at which such a statement is indeed true, so that the only thing that remains for us to do is to give thanks to God. And in that thanksgiving we are in him and with him in his Kingdom, because there is now nothing else left, because that is where our ascension has already led us.[29]

28. Schmemann, "Liturgy and Eschatology," 11.

29. Schmemann, "Liturgy and Eschatology," 11. Here, Calvin would concur with the point made, except that Schmemann widens the scope of the church's "ascension" to the presence of Christ to worship in general and not just during the Lord's Supper. There is, of course, no

In his book *A Third Testament*, Malcolm Muggeridge looks into the lives of seven leading Christians who made an impact on their society within the respective time period they lived in. Muggeridge says of them, "Considering them as a group, it became clear to me that, although they were all quintessentially men of their time, they had a special role in common, which was none other than to relate their time to eternity."[30] What he says of them is a fitting description of what the church should be also. As those who have entered the eighth day of creation through the weekly Lord's Day communion with God, our sense of *kairos* time has been sharpened again. And we are in a position once more to demonstrate how *kairos* time should be lived in the midst of *chronos* time. We can become witnesses again through our words and deeds of the glorious providence that God has for humanity through the eighth day of creation.

The Church's Doctrine of Providence as a Tomorrowland Portal

After years of going to Disneyland, I noticed something very strange about Tomorrowland. Either for lack of financial resources or scientific data or both, it seems as if Tomorrowland has lost its ability to be futuristic. Somehow, every time I go there, I no longer sense that a bit of the future is being brought to the present or that I am being transported to the future. In fact, it seems as if the world outside Tomorrowland is far more advanced and capable of depicting the future. Why has Tomorrowland lost its ability to be proleptic about the future?

Pat Williams, a biographer of Walt Disney, shed some light on this matter. He says, "After Walt's death in 1966, his Imagineers faced the challenge of keeping Tomorrowland fresh and forward-looking. As the world changed, the task grew increasingly more complex. Tomorrowland attractions of the 1950s looked quaintly archaic by the 1970s."[31] Instead of keeping up with what the future is revealing to us through science, in the late 1990s Disneyland decided to turn Tomorrowland into a historic

seeming contradiction between Schmemann's and Calvin's views of the church's ascension to the presence of Christ during corporate worship, since the Lord's Supper would naturally be inclusive of proper liturgy of worship for both theologians.

30. Muggeridge, *A Third Testament*, v.

31. Williams, *How to Be like Walt*, 239.

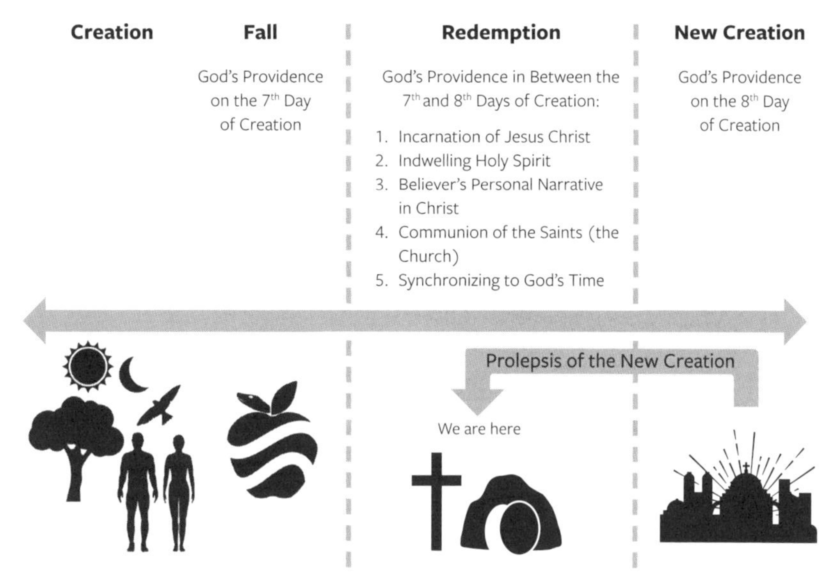

Figure 7.1

preserve of what it was supposed to be back in heyday of Disneyland. By doing it this way, "Tomorrowland can retain its nostalgic-futuristic charm for decades to come—and that will save the Disney company millions in remodeling costs."[32]

Williams then asked the penetrating question, "Would Walt approve?" His initial response was, "I'm not sure." But then he goes on to be more forthright in saying, "Walt would probably mourn the loss of a truly futuristic dimension to Disneyland. The new Tomorrowland no longer gives us a window on 'new frontiers in science,' or on 'the challenge of outer space.'"[33]

There is a parallel between the church and Tomorrowland. Both have been tasked by their respective founders to help those who come to them experience aspects of the future. It is understandable—though sad and tragic—that when Walt Disney died, Tomorrowland lost its vision and ability to provide a prolepsis of the future to its patrons. But the obsolescence of Tomorrowland need not happen to the church. As chapters 5

32. Williams, *How to Be like Walt*, 239.
33. Williams, *How to Be like Walt*, 239.

and 6 have shown, the church can thrive as it continues to proclaim and embody the importance of

- the incarnation of Jesus Christ
- the indwelling Holy Spirit
- the believer's new narrative in Christ
- the communion of the saints
- the synchronization to God's time

For God the Father has given the church not just the doctrine of providence inscribed in the Bible, but a risen Savior, Jesus Christ, whom the doctrine proclaims as the portal to the eighth day of creation. There can be a continuous prolepsis of that glorious future today through the power of his Holy Spirit. And the church can be the conduit of this prolepsis; it can be an eighth-day community for a world dying to know and experience God's good providence about the future.

8

Providence Reframed

Frames are the Cinderellas of the art world; they do a tremendous amount of work.

—Emma Crichton-Miller, "What Goes Around: The Art of Framing"

The essence of every picture is the frame.

—G. K. Chesterton, Orthodoxy

When veteran actor and comedian Bill Murray was still a struggling young artist living in Chicago, he was so bad in his craft that one day he decided to just end his life. He determined to do it in the waters of Lake Michigan. Walking toward the lake, on a whim, he decided to make a side trip to the local art museum, the Art Institute of Chicago. There he happened upon the nineteenth-century painting of Jules Breton entitled *The Song of the Lark*, depicting a peasant girl working in a field at sunrise while pausing to listen to the lark singing.

This masterpiece moved Bill Murray so much that he pondered deeply about life. He says, "I just thought, 'Well, look there's a girl who doesn't have a whole lot of prospects, but the sun is coming up anyway and she's

Figure 8.1 *The Song of the Lark* (1884) by Jules Breton

got another chance at it.' And I think that made me think, 'I too am a person. And I get another chance every day the sun comes up.'" With that inspirational insight from *The Song of the Lark*, he decided to forgo his attempt to commit suicide. It can be safely said that this painting hanging in the gallery of the Art Institute of Chicago saved Bill Murray's life that day.[1]

1. "Bill Murray Admits a Painting Saved His Life," YouTube video, 2:40, posted by Red Carpet News TV, February 11, 2014, https://youtu.be/8eOIcWB7jSA.

Art masterpieces have a way of doing profound things like that to us. But they cannot speak to us deeply and transformatively unless they are made accessible to the public, as in a museum, and presented winsomely, as in an art gallery. Bill Murray's life could not have been saved by *The Song of the Lark* if the painting were kept in some private cellar or its canvas rolled up in the corner of a museum. In short, the art masterpiece had to be framed and displayed in a proper setting for it to do its work effectively, such as on the day Bill Murray came into the museum with his troubles.

The doctrine of providence is like an art masterpiece as well. (Indeed, it is better than a painting.) It is able to speak to us deeply and transformatively. But for that to happen, it too must be communicated in an accessible and winsome way. In short, God's masterpiece of the doctrine of providence must be framed properly in the museum of public discourse. What I have proposed to do in this book is to reframe the doctrine of providence through the theological frame of the seventh and eighth days of creation. The intent for this reframing is so that the doctrine of providence's masterpiece quality might better speak to troubled souls who are looking for God's consolation.

The Need for a New Frame

A great Bible expositor of yesteryear, D. Martyn Lloyd-Jones, once made this rather bold and surprising statement: "I am prepared to assert that perhaps in this twentieth century of ours the most important doctrine in many ways is the doctrine of providence."[2] He quickly added, though, that it's not because providence is any more important than other doctrines, such as the incarnation or the atonement. Rather, it's because the doctrine of providence is "the stumbling-block to a large number of people who are outside Christ and outside the Church."[3] The complaints that people made in the time of Lloyd-Jones that gave rise to the need to focus on this doctrine were these:

> They say, "I cannot believe your doctrine, I cannot believe your gospel. You say that God is a God of love, well, look at the world; look at the things that have happened in the world; look at these two world wars! How can you reconcile

2. Lloyd-Jones, *Great Doctrines of the Bible*, 141.
3. Lloyd-Jones, *Great Doctrines of the Bible*, 141.

> something like that with a God of love, a God who you say is all-powerful, so powerful that there is nothing He cannot do if He so chooses? How can you explain all this?" So you see, the very historical situation in this century concentrates attention immediately upon this great doctrine of providence.[4]

How little has changed since the time of Lloyd-Jones! If anything, the criticisms that he cites coming from non-Christian quarters have now even extended to Christian quarters. Chapter 1 has sufficiently demonstrated this problem. Thus, an argument can be made that, all the more in the twenty-first century, there has to be a concerted and persuasive effort to make clear and compelling the doctrine of providence so that a new generation might benefit from it.

Apparently, the previous ways of articulating the doctrine of providence have not fully resolved the concerns that Lloyd-Jones and others have sought to address in their lifetime, and the problem has now even spilled over to our present time and to our present churches. Why? As stated in the preface of this book, it's because of what Charles Taylor calls "the immanent frame," which denies any notion of transcendence in human flourishing and instead regards societal progress strictly from the standpoint of human self-effort.

How can this frame be changed? What novel way of communicating the doctrine of providence can be used to achieve the desired result? This book has employed an approach that is not novel, but ancient, to communicate the doctrine of providence. It has used the seventh and eighth days of creation as a frame to reframe the doctrine.

Like a masterpiece painting, the doctrine of providence as revealed in the pages of Scripture needs no retouching from theologians. The Word of God speaks for itself. But where theologians can be helpful is by putting the masterpiece of the doctrine of providence in a frame that is suitable for this present generation to understand and appreciate the masterpiece. One might say that it is time for theologians to consider whether the present theological frame that holds the biblical portrait of providence needs reexamining for its effectiveness.

In the art world, frames play an important role in setting up the audience for the masterpiece's appreciation. As Emma Crichton-Miller colorfully says,

4. Lloyd-Jones, *Great Doctrines of the Bible*, 141.

> Frames are the Cinderellas of the art world; they do a tremendous amount of work. They protect the artworks they support; they show off the qualities of a picture, drawing attention to its formal structure, its patterns and colours, enabling them to resonate fully with a viewer; they mould the response of the viewer to the work by suggesting the value we should attach to it; they accommodate a painting to its setting, acting as a liaison between the dream world of art and the decorative scheme of the museum, gallery or private home the work inhabits. They are partly furniture and partly sculpture. At their best, they are works of art, carved by the foremost sculptors of their day, and yet their own brilliance must also serve that of the paintings they encase.[5]

The seventh and eighth days of creation approach is just that: a theological frame for the masterpiece of the doctrine of providence to do its work in the lives of readers.

The Four Sides of a New Frame for the Doctrine of Providence

Like any portrait, though, the seventh and eighth days of creation approach to providence also has four sides to it. These four sides of its theological frame are characterized as

- dramatic
- existential
- boundary-setting
- invitational

In this book's final chapter, the doctrine of providence is reprised along the lines of its reframed portrait.

The Dramatic Side of the Frame

John Webster points out that there are two basic tasks in the work of theologizing: expounding and disputing.[6] The former seeks to explain, while

5. Crichton-Miller, "What Goes Around."

6. John Webster describes the first task as *expositio*, "an analytic-expository task, in which it attempts orderly conceptual representation of the content of the Christian gospel as it is

the latter seeks to persuade. Webster wisely observes that disputation must be subordinate to exposition. For when we focus merely on disputing with critics on a theological issue, we unwittingly fail to explain the cogency and the beauty of a theological point, which is what makes Christian theology naturally compelling. Webster suggests that this is, indeed, what has happened to the doctrine of providence.[7] The order of its presentation has been reversed. Unfortunately, the emphasis has been disputation before exposition. Consequently, the doctrine has lost much of its persuasive power among those who inquire about God's providence.

While in agreement with Webster, I would add a corollary to his wise theological method. When theologizing, exposition must not just be preeminent over disputation but must also include demonstration (i.e., the exhibition of the theological truth). In other words, theology must not only exposit theological truths but must also exhibit the beauty and the relevance of the theological truth in such a way that appeals to the whole person, not just his or her analytic mind. So, here's a simple maxim. When discussing the doctrine of providence, inasmuch as possible, demonstrate; do not dispute. Show, rather than argue, the theological point. As goes the advice to young writers, "Don't tell me the moon is shining; show me the glint of light on broken glass." When we present the doctrine of providence as demonstration, we make it compelling to readers and listeners.

But how do we do the work of demonstration? What do we highlight in the vast corpus of the Bible? One way the doctrine of providence can be expounded and demonstrated so as to become compelling is by using the dramatic aspects found in the motif of the seventh and eighth days of creation. The motif is dramatic because it shows God acting and inviting us to participate in his work in the seventh and eighth days of creation. For instance, when the thorny theological issue of divine sovereignty and human free will creeps up in the midst of an exposition of the doctrine of providence and threatens to turn it into an ugly disputation, the proper demonstration of the drama found within the seventh and eighth days of creation turns the discussion back to its proper edifying focus. This

laid out in the scriptural witnesses." The second is *disputatio*, "a polemical apologetic task in which it explores the justification and value of Christian truth claims." Webster, *God without Measure*, 30.

7. Webster, *God without Measure*, 127–28.

approach bypasses the need for an in-depth disputation in discussing the doctrine, for it simply and dramatically demonstrates the compelling love of a sovereign God to rescue humanity and, thereby, sets up the human need to respond accordingly to him throughout their existence.

Citing approvingly Hans Urs von Balthasar's *Theo-drama*, Kevin Vanhoozer articulates how drama can help resolve the ongoing issue of the problem of divine sovereignty and human freedom in providence:

> The problem with the human condition is not metaphysical, an implication of finitude, but spiritual, an implication of fallenness. Similarly, the message of the gospel is neither metaphysical or moral, but dramatic: God himself speaks and acts in order to end the conflict between human and divine freedom.[8]

Vanhoozer further says,

> The drama of redemption is thus a great twofold odyssey, in which humanity, along with the rest of creation, loses its way and finds its way home only because God leaves home in order to bring everyone back. The Scriptures depict a covenantal drama moved forward by the love of God. . . . [The dramatic aspect of the d]octrine preserves this dynamic thrust by drawing us into the action of what God is doing in Jesus Christ.[9]

Whereas the "immanent frame" of secularization centers the drama of life on the self and human capability, the motif of the seventh and eighth days of creation for the doctrine of providence shows that the dramatic aspect of life centers on the triune God of the Bible. If life were a movie or a play, God would be the protagonist and humanity his supporting cast. The "twofold odyssey" that Vanhoozer refers to easily corresponds to the motif of the seventh and eighth days of creation that this book traces. The seventh day is essentially the time when humanity lost their way home, and the eighth day is essentially God leaving his home to bring everyone back. This dramatic aspect not only is faithful to the biblical metanarrative; it also speaks to the kind of knowledge that satisfies the longing of the human soul when it comes to providence.

8. Vanhoozer, *Drama of Doctrine*, 50.
9. Vanhoozer, *Drama of Doctrine*, 55–56.

On the seventh day of creation God rested in order to make room for creatures he created to act out their supporting role in the drama of life. Citing John Calvin, Karl Barth reminds us that humanity is the theater of God's glory:

> It is not God's fault if we do not feel at home in our creatureliness and in this creaturely world. This is a notion which can obtrude only if we suspend as it were our faith in God's providence and do not take seriously our membership of the kingdom of Christ. If we take this seriously, our eyes are open to the fact that the created world including our own existence fulfils that purpose and constitutes that *theatrum gloriae Dei*. It and we are present in order that God may have time, space and opportunity to pursue in the history of the covenant of grace the work which is the goal of His creative will and to hasten towards which He has made it His own most proper cause with the interposition of Himself in Jesus Christ.[10]

In short, this motif sets a theocentric dramatic tone to the doctrine of providence. Or, to put it bluntly, in the words of Rick Warren, "It is not about you."[11] It's about God. Centered on the actions and words of the triune God, one cannot help but change the immanent frame of humanity to the dramatic frame of God.

Such a perspective has a way of changing the way we approach the doctrine of providence not just from *disputatio* to *expositio* but, ultimately, to *doxologia*. And when our mindset is doxological, it is safe to say that the way we treat the subject of providence, with all its complexities, takes on a different attitude: a more humble and worshipful one, from which true understanding and life transformation will come.

The Existential Side of the Frame

In his book *Critique of Pure Reason*, Immanuel Kant famously states,

> All interest of my reason (the speculative as well as the practical) is united in the following three questions:

10. Barth, *Church Dogmatics*, 46–47.
11. Warren, *Purpose-Driven Life*, 17.

1. What can I know?
2. What should I do?
3. What may I hope?[12]

With good reason did Kant isolate these three key questions, for they comprise crucial issues salient to human existence. Lacking a satisfactory response to them, life is not worth living. If the reframed doctrine of providence is to capture the imagination of inquirers, then its existential value has to be demonstrated in its response to these questions. Thus, without necessarily agreeing with Kant's premise or his responses to them, I would like to address the existential side of the reframed doctrine of providence using these three questions.

1. What Can I Know?

The motif of the seventh and eighth days of creation provides us with the most basic but of utmost important knowledge: the knowledge of oneself. It reveals to us that we are partners of a loving and sovereign Lord who created us to rule this world with him. Despite our straying away from him into sin, he continues to sustain (preserve) us and to use us in the care of his creation. This is the seventh day of the creation account of humanity. Karl Barth calls this "the history of creation"[13] or "cosmic history."[14]

But God's providence exceeds the original creation. He promises another day of creation in which he will once again take up *creatio ex nihilo* in the form of the new creation. That day is designated by the early church as the eighth day of creation. This day reveals to us the truth that humanity remains God's creation partner. The big difference is that, on that day, we and the entire world will be reconstituted so as to make the divine-human partnership no longer hindered by sin and its effects. While this eighth day of creation is yet future, interestingly and paradoxically,

12. Kant, *Critique of Pure Reason*, 677.

13. Barth, *Church Dogmatics*, 6, 45. It does not seem that Barth fuses the seventh and eighth days of the creation account. He seems to see the seventh day as the beginning of the eighth day. While the terminology may differ, my view is not far different in essence from Barth's since the "already" aspect of the eighth day is occurring at the tail end of the seventh day of creation even as it is transitioning into the eighth day.

14. Barth, *Church Dogmatics*, 46.

it also runs parallel with the seventh day of creation time frame.[15] Karl Barth calls this "the history of the covenant"—that is, "of the covenant of grace"[16]—and also "the history of salvation."[17]

All humanity can find in the seventh day of creation their self-identity as partners of God for creation care. It is the dignity given to every human being that God created. But believers in Christ have one added identity marker that propels them to a greater participation in creation care. By virtue of their union with Christ, believers have entered into the eighth day of creation that Christ inaugurated through his incarnation. Thus, believers have not only a self-identity as God's creation partner but also a new and intimate narrative. It is the narrative that all that is Christ's is now ours also. We have a new narrative as children of God through Christ. We are heirs of God and coheirs with Christ. This new personal and intimate story is not only affirming but also, more importantly, purpose-generating in one's daily living. It is a self-knowledge that elevates the quality of our living and participation in God's calling. As Alasdair MacIntyre says, "I can only answer the question, 'What am I to do?' if I can answer the prior question 'Of what story or stories do I find myself a part?'"[18]

2. *What Should I Do?*

The existential question of what I should do has, in a sense, been addressed in the previous discussion on self-knowledge. What a person should do is anything that is consistent with what God has revealed concerning his or her identity as God's partner. There is a wideness and freedom of choice as far as this vocational task is concerned. To go back to the metaphor of the drama of redemption, we see that God has provided the means for his supporting cast to do their part with the kind of dependent freedom befitting such creatures. What follows, then, is that the "created cosmos including man, or man within the created cosmos, is this theatre of the great acts of God in grace and salvation."[19] And as Barth nicely expounds,

15. Barth, *Church Dogmatics*, 45–51.
16. Barth, *Church Dogmatics*, 6, 45, 47.
17. Barth, *Church Dogmatics*, 46.
18. MacIntyre, *After Virtue*, 216.
19. Barth, *Church Dogmatics*, 46.

> Provision has been and is continually made for this theatre of the history of the covenant of grace, for time, space and opportunity for the divine work of grace and salvation. It tells us that this provision is made by God Himself. It speaks of the specific and as it were supplementary divine work of this provision. There will be time, space and opportunity for the history of the covenant of grace, for faith, knowledge, repentance, love and hope, until this history reaches its divinely appointed end. In great and little things alike all this will be continually furnished by the sustaining and overruling sway of God as the Lord of heaven and earth. This is the divine co-ordination and integration of cosmic history with the history of salvation.[20]

As in the garden of Eden, the work is plentiful in the vast world that God created. There is no one right or wrong place to begin. But wherever one begins, the issue comes down to whether or not that person can work with the kind of integrity God expects. In other words, perhaps, the existential question is not so much "What should I do?" as "What should I do so that I can do what I should do?"

Here, on a deeper level, we are dealing with the reality that there are obstacles that keep us from doing what we should. Two such obstacles in particular are our creaturely limitations and our sinful disposition. These keep us from doing what we should. Until they are properly addressed, there is little point asking, "What should I do?" For very little of what we are created for by God will be done under these preexisting conditions.

The motif of the seventh and eighth days of creation helpfully provides us with God's providential response to the preexisting conditions. With regard to our human creatureliness, God does not remove our creatureliness, such as the need for food and rest. But he promises to provide for his creatures all that they need according to his good purposes. The Sabbath day command to rest, rooted in the seventh day of creation, is a good example of an actual and a symbolic provision. On this day, Israel had to stop and get their literal rest so as to actually benefit from it. But every time Israel responded by resting on the Sabbath, despite perhaps having an important matter to attend to, they learned the deeper symbolic lesson of Sabbath, which is to trust in God's provision by intentionally leaning not on human effort but on God.

20. Barth, *Church Dogmatics*, 46.

As for the sinful disposition, the motif of the seventh day of creation shows that God has provided his Word, which reveals himself, his ways, and his promises to his people as a means of combating sin and its effects. As Paul observes in Romans, there is great advantage in having the oracles of God (Rom. 3:1–2). Moreover, the Holy Spirit is always at work to restrain sin and even to overcome sin so as to produce the blessings that humanity constantly enjoys. This is called common grace. However, it is safe to say that the provision of the seventh day of creation is not all that God intended to provide for humanity. Even people in the Old Testament yearned for more of God's provision in the form of an eighth day of creation. And God did promise to give humanity an eighth day of creation blessing.

The motif of the eighth day of creation represents the culmination of God's providential blessing to humankind. For here, both the creaturely limitation and sinful incapacity are dealt with completely. Those who enter into the eighth day of creation will ultimately, but even now to a degree, be able to overcome their creaturely limitation and sinful incapacity. In the future, believers will be resurrected and be given the same glorified body as that of Jesus Christ. At that time, God will purge this created order of sin so that we can dwell in it with our resurrected bodies unhindered by sin, ruling the created order together with Christ just as God had always intended for us to do when he created humanity.

In the meantime, however, the eighth day is not just for the future. It carries with it present-day benefits and effects: the power to live out God's calling in our lives. God has given those who are in Christ the gift of the Holy Spirit in order that they might appropriate "the power of the age to come" today (Heb. 6:5). This is why believers can live out aspects of the eighth day today. They can truly ask, "What should I do?" and have the proper provision of power from God to execute their required tasks without fail, all things being equal. This eighth-day gift is the gospel message that believers are to proclaim and demonstrate to those around them as part of their responsibility as God's partners of caring for creation.

3. What May I Hope?

In a world searching for hope, the motif of the seventh and eighth days of creation lays out a message of hope to frame the doctrine of providence.

To be sure, this hope is seen in the daily divine provision for our needs. It allowed Sam Polk (see chap. 2) to do the daring deed of leaving a high-paying job with the confidence that "the universe" would still provide for his needs. God graciously provided for Sam Polk's needs despite his failure to even acknowledge God. But this provision would constitute merely the preservation of the existing order.

Biblical providence, however, is not just "preservation" but also "governance." It portrays a God who has the ultimate good of his creation and his glory in mind and then executes his will accordingly. In other words, the hope found in the motif of the seventh and eighth days of creation is teleological in nature. It has in view the complete plan of God's purposes for the world. John Webster helpfully points out,

> A Christian doctrine of Providence is only derivatively a theory of history, the cosmology or an account of divine action in the world; most properly it is a representation of how the Father's plan for the fullness of time is set forth in Christ and made actual by the Holy Spirit among the children of Adam.[21]

Thus, he adds, "Providence is not mere static world maintenance but teleological, the fulfillment of the ordered fellowship with God which is the creature's perfected happiness."[22] In short, the full panoply of hope that God's plan generates cannot be fully seen or appreciated without taking into account the climax of the eighth day of creation. God's goodness and love for creation cannot be properly evaluated and experienced without considering its end result.

What this means, according to Colin Gunton, is that "providence must be understood eschatologically, from the end."[23] The way we do theology in general and explicate providence in particular must include eschatology if our treatment of these matters is to be thoroughly complete. Indeed, this is how the early church always theologized.[24] Gunton goes on to say, "God's providential purposes are realized only eschatologically, and that means, first of all, only through time; the creation needs time to be and to become

21. Webster, *God without Measure*, 131.
22. Webster, *God without Measure*, 131.
23. Gunton, *Christian Faith*, 36.
24. Blowers, *Drama of the Divine Economy*.

itself."[25] What Gunton says carries important implications for the way we do *disputatio* with critics and how we move forward existentially in hope.

To the critics who raise, for instance, the problem of evil, the best response is to simply say that God's providential purposes are realized eschatologically—that is, through time. In time, all these questions will be answered sufficiently. And if one is unable to wait for the passage of time, then one will have to leap in front of time toward the end with the eyes of faith and with the aid of divine revelation to get a sense of what God's good purposes are for his creation even in the face of evil. But, presently, God simply will not and cannot allow himself to be cajoled by critics, just to provide them with an answer, to move events faster than what he has planned through the instrumentality of time.

For those who look for hope, the motif of the seventh and eighth days of creation presents eschatological hope. While yet future, the beauty of the eighth day of creation is that it is not confined merely in the eschaton. There is an "already" aspect of the eighth day of creation that makes hope something to expect ahead but also something to be inhabited now. Through the ministry of the gift of the Holy Spirit we can have a foretaste of that which we are hoping for in the eschaton. That makes the Christian hope something that is tangible today despite being conditioned upon the future for its full benefit. As Gunton explains, "Yet because eschatological time bears now upon created time, the purposes of the creator are ever and again realized, in advance, so far as we are concerned, as people and things are enabled to be that which they were made to be."[26] This makes then for a hope that is both future and present, both potentiality and reality. Truly, the existential value of this frame is immensely accessible and life transformative now.

Although there is a lot of tangible hope to speak of and experience, one must not overstate the fact that the bulk of the Christian hope in divine providence is truly yet future. Not to recognize this leads not only to disillusionment but also, worse, to a life of ease and inability to endure the hardships associated with living the radical Christian life. The Christian life is not an escape from the present difficulty of a present fallen world. It is to this fallen world that believers are called by God to bring their

25. Gunton, *Christian Faith*, 36.
26. Gunton, *Christian Faith*, 36.

message of hope in Christ through proclamation and practical life demonstration. The reality, though, is that people's response to such a message and lifestyle is inhospitable and often hostile. Without the steadfastness of eschatological future hope, one's willingness to suffer hardship in the face of trial, even to the point of death or martyrdom, would wane. But holding on to this future hope creates the desired effect of faithful discipleship.

God is not the only actor in the theater of God's glory. Believers have a role also. Part of what makes their role dramatic is how they respond to their divine calling (who they are and what they should do). An aid to their faithful discharge of their role can be found in the hope generated by the motif of the seventh and eighth days of creation. When the eschaton finally arrives, the prophet Isaiah depicts believers' drama grounded in hope this way:

> Now the LORD of hosts will prepare a lavish banquet for all
> peoples on this mountain;
> A banquet of aged wine, choice pieces with marrow,
> And refined, aged wine.
> And on this mountain He will destroy the covering which is over all
> peoples,
> Even the veil which is stretched over all nations.
> He will swallow up death for all time,
> And the Lord GOD will wipe tears away from all faces,
> And He will remove the reproach of His people from all the earth;
> For the LORD has spoken.
> And it will be said on that day,
> "Behold, this is our God for whom we have waited that He might
> save us.
> This is the LORD for whom we have waited;
> Let us rejoice and be glad in His salvation." (Isa. 25:6–9)

The Boundary-Setting Side of the Frame

This chapter shows that the reframed doctrine of providence along the lines of the motif of the seventh and eighth days of creation has explanatory power that affects and transforms lives. But, like any picture frame, the theological frame of the seventh and eighth days of creation also serves to set the boundary of how much we can see and ought to see in the masterpiece without overstating what the artist would have us to see. For as G. K. Chesterton wisely observes, "Art is limitation; the essence of a picture is its frame."[27] He goes on to explain,

> If you draw a giraffe, you must draw him with a long neck. If, in your bold creative way, you hold yourself free to draw a giraffe with a short neck, you will really find that you are not free to draw a giraffe. . . . This is certainly the case with all artistic creation, which is in some ways the most decisive example of pure will. The artist loves his limitations: they constitute the *thing* he is doing.[28]

Theologians, as artistic framers of the Bible's doctrinal masterpieces, likewise know their limits. The best of them are sensitive to the natural boundaries involved in the whole theological endeavor.

The Bible is replete with these natural limits to what theologians can say about its great subject matters. Paradoxes, mysteries, and supernatural occurrences attributable to the divine are just some clear examples of these limits contained in Scripture. Theologians will be wise to respect the natural boundaries found therein. Any attempts to breach the gap between the divine and the human could result in doctrinal disaster with unpleasant spiritual and existential consequences.

One such teaching close to the subject of providence is God's relationship to evil. It is always tempting to incorporate evil into the sphere of the divine so as to assert God's complete sovereignty over evil. Such a move makes logical sense. Interestingly, however, Scripture forbids such an attempt. The apostle James writes,

> Let no one say when he is tempted, "I am being tempted by God"; for God cannot be tempted by evil, and He Himself does not tempt anyone. But each one is tempted when he is carried away and enticed by his own lust. Then when lust has conceived, it gives birth to sin; and when sin is accomplished, it brings forth death. Do not be deceived, my beloved brethren. Every good thing given and every perfect gift is from above, coming down from the Father of lights, with whom there is no variation or shifting shadow. (James 1:13–17)

27. Chesterton, *Orthodoxy*, 45.
28. Chesterton, *Orthodoxy*, 45–46.

There is, therefore, a theological boundary or frame on the subject of God and evil such that no logic can fuse the two together.

The Boundary for Concursus

In the doctrine of providence, the matter of concursus is a theological issue that needs to be handled with great boundary-setting care. "Concursus" means "an aspect of God's Providence whereby he cooperates with created things in every action, directing their distinctive properties to cause them to act as they do."[29] By this definition, everything in God's creation falls within his concurrence. But what does that mean? How does that work? The difficulty is in the details.

No matter how we choose to tackle concursus, John Webster helpfully reminds us that we should properly frame "the canonical portrait of the Lord of the covenant"[30] so that an accurate picture of him gets highlighted. In descriptions of God's action in concursus, he sometimes is depicted as the God not of the Bible but of natural theology or mere logical theology.

How, then, should we properly portray God's work in concursus? Without denying that God moves all things to act according to his will and purposes, Webster counsels that "we strip the notion of 'moving' of any abstract ideas of sheer causal force" that end up depicting God as less than who is portrayed in the canon of Scripture—that is, as a mere impersonal force.[31] Kevin Vanhoozer maintains that we are to "let the material content of what the Bible says about the nature of God's sovereign power govern one's understanding of causality."[32] Additionally, when discussing divine concurrence, Webster insists that we should "show how the freedom and

29. Grudem, *Systematic Theology*, 1238.

30. Webster, *God without Measure*, 139. Webster lays out a good rule of thumb for the proper discussion of divine causality in providence: "That a theological metaphysics of divine action is required is unquestionable (without it, belief in Providence shrinks to a subjective disposition); but the metaphysics must follow the confession which it explicates, and so take some care to register the fact that words such as 'motion' or 'cause' are ministerial and not principle" (137).

31. Webster, *God without Measure*, 139.

32. Vanhoozer, *Remythologizing Theology*, 369. Citing Barth approvingly, Vanhoozer further says, "Barth is willing to speak of God's causality provided that what it describes is not some abstract absolute power but 'the operation of the Father of Jesus Christ in relation to that of the creature.' He therefore identifies God's agency not with the general concept of a mechanical cause but with the unique and particular causality of covenantal grace. God's control of the world in general is a by-product of his loving concern for his covenant people." Vanhoozer, *Remythologizing Theology*, 369, citing Barth, *Church Dogmatics* III/3, 105.

dignity of creatures are caught up, not suppressed or eliminated by, the rule of God."[33]

But is such a thing possible? Can God's act of moving the human will render the human action as free? Quoting Aquinas, Webster answers, "Yes, because 'to be moved voluntarily is to be moved of one's own accord, i.e., from a resource within. That inner resource, however, may derive from some other, outward source. In this sense, there is no contradiction between being moved of one's own accord and being moved by another.'"[34] Webster says that "divine providential acts are not simple compulsion (the archer sending the arrow)," but rather are "intrinsic" to the nature of creatures; God taps into what Aquinas calls their sense of "natural necessity" to move them to action. [35] By this, God may have activated creatures to act without diminishing their dignity as decision-making creatures, since the action was their own.

Agreeing with Webster, Vanhoozer observes that the "Christian doctrine of providence will not be content with conceiving God as one who unilaterally moves people about like so many otherwise inert chess pieces. That way fatalism lies. But neither does God let the pieces take control of the board." Vanhoozer proposes instead that God's strong work of concurrence on the chess board of human existence be seen as "God convincingly persuades some of the pieces freely to play of their own accord in a way that so corresponds to God's will that we can speak (albeit hesitantly) in terms of dual agency."[36] In other words, no matter how influential God's concurrence is, it is persuasive in nature, not coercive. "It is in such dialogical interaction that we best see the way in which God exercises his sovereignty and humans their freedom."[37] In short, for Vanhoozer, this is the way concursus is understood within the context of providence: "Divine providence is best viewed in terms of triune authorship: *the Father rules by speaking Christ through the Spirit into the minds and hearts of the faithful*."[38]

In both Webster's and Vanhoozer's approaches to concursus, one thing noticeable is that both speak of God's causality in providence in a

33. Webster, *God without Measure*, 139.
34. Webster, *God without Measure*, 139, quoting Aquinas, *Summa theologiae* I.105.4 ad.
35. Webster, *God without Measure*, 139.
36. Vanhoozer, *Remythologizing Theology*, 367.
37. Vanhoozer, *Remythologizing Theology*, 367.
38. Vanhoozer, *Remythologizing Theology*, 376.

"limited" or biblically bounded way. There is a measured way in which they discuss concursus so that it does not become naturalistic or speculative but remains faithful to all the theological concerns related in the subject matter. Neither of them goes into specifics of causality that seek to explain the "causal joints."

This boundary-setting approach is also what is demonstrated in this book's approach to the doctrine of providence. For the motif of the seventh and eighth days of creation is essentially grounded in the metanarrative of the Bible comprising of creation, fall, redemption, and new creation. There is a narratival connection between the seventh and eighth days of God's creation providence. But not all the divine causes, as well as divine and human causal interaction, are explained thoroughly by design, given the inherent theological and spiritual limitations. Furthermore, conceptual discussions of God's actions in providence are seen in light of the Father's two hands: the Son and the Spirit. It is in this sense, therefore, that this approach to providence has a boundary-setting frame to it.

The Boundary for Reprobation (Double Predestination)

When contemplating providence, one's thought does not just turn to those who benefit from God's loving provision—the positive outcome of divine providence. It also turns to the other group, those who have not benefited from God's loving providence—the negative outcome of divine providence. The issue here is not whether the latter group was given a chance to respond or receive God's provision, especially in the form of ultimate salvation in Jesus Christ. The question is this: Did God have something to do with their final outcome of rejecting his work of providence in their life? And, if so, in what way was God's providence responsible for such a negative outcome? This issue before us is often referred to as that of reprobation. And so the topic of double predestination inevitably arises within this discussion.

The issue seems to be addressed straightforwardly by James 1:13–17, mentioned above. That should provide a boundary for how this issue is pursued. And yet, not all theologians are satisfied to just let that text have the last word.

Emil Brunner, in *The Christian Doctrine of God*, mentions John Calvin as someone who, as far as the matter of reprobation is concerned, fell into the trap of pursuing a theological line of thought when he should have stopped. Calvin's persistence landed him in the view of double predestination, which upholds God's sovereignty over the destiny of all but also renders him responsible for their state of reprobation. Although he acknowledges that Calvin never preached on double predestination, Brunner says,

> Calvin fails to perceive the real origin of this doctrine of double predestination—that is, speculative natural theology—from the application of the causal concept to unbelief—owing to the fact that he believes that he has derived his doctrine entirely from the Holy Scriptures, in that he combines certain Bible passages with one another—no one of which really contains this doctrine—in such a way that, together, they appeared to provide the scriptural proof for the *gemini praedestinatio*.[39]

Brunner proceeds to show that Martin Luther, in his early career, also shared a view very similar to Calvin's. What is indisputable is that later in life Luther changed his view of double predestination so much so that his mature view on this issue becomes a dividing and distinguishing line between Lutherans and Calvinists.

What happened? According to Brunner, "The decisive turning point in Luther's thought" comes in 1525 when he "warned his hearers against seeking for a hidden divine decree."[40] Luther says, "No one ought to dispute about the '*nuda Divinitatis*' [that is, about the will of God that has not been revealed], but we ought to flee from such thoughts as from Hell itself, and as from temptations of the devil."[41] Brunner explains, "Luther perceives that the question of [double] predestination lies outside the sphere of Christian revelation and of faith, and that it is a question of speculative natural theology. It is the scholastic speculative theology which makes the distinction between a '*voluntas signi*' (the revealed will) and the '*voluntas beniplaticiti*,' the unsearchable divine election or rejection."[42]

Luther, therefore, has drawn his boundary of doing his theology strictly along the lines of the revealed God and his Word. Whatever else is unknown

39. Brunner, *Christian Doctrine of God*, 343.
40. Brunner, *Christian Doctrine of God*, 343.
41. Quoted in Brunner, *Christian Doctrine of God*, 343–44.
42. Brunner, *Christian Doctrine of God*, 343.

about God and his will that he has not revealed in Jesus Christ, it is of no concern to him. He would be content to remain silent on those things and focus on the clearly revealed will of God.

The contrasting approach between two towering giants of the Reformation serves as our paradigm on how to handle the contours of the doctrine of providence.[43] This book's approach follows Luther in drawing the boundary in the same line of demarcation that he drew. This does not mean that double predestination could not be discussed, but it does mean that such discussion will not have the same level of importance and sense of urgency as do other theological issues clearly revealed in the Word of God. In so doing, the motif of the seventh and eighth days of creation maintains a proper theological boundary on the portrait of God's divine providence.

The Invitational Side of the Frame

Like any art masterpiece, God's masterpiece of the doctrine of providence does not simply inform its audience but also inspires them to respond. There is an invitational quality to the masterpiece of providence. It calls those who come in contact with it to participate in the great message it carries. How should this invitation be framed? To use an old and yet contemporarily well-known watchword, *carpe diem*—in today's common parlance, "Seize the day!"[44] If, indeed, God has revealed his providence

43. This comment is intended not to put down John Calvin but merely to compare the theological methodology of the two Reformers and to commend Martin Luther's approach. Calvin is often quite balanced in his treatment of determinism. However, there are occasions in his writings where he can be perceived to tilt toward double predestination. Perhaps he is zealously teasing out certain scriptural implications when he does so. Rightly or wrongly, theologians such as Emil Brunner criticize him for his close proximity to double predestination. In my reading of his works, however, I do not believe that, in the aggregate, double predestination is the hallmark of John Calvin's theology, any more than it is Martin Luther's hallmark just because he wrote *On the Bondage of the Will*. For a more nuanced discussion on John Calvin and double predestination, see Hesselink, "Calvin's Theology," 83–84.

44. To say *carpe diem* in our society is to use shorthand to communicate something very powerful and urgent. It conjures up certain images of how life is to be lived. Despite the popularity of this Latin phrase, scholars debate its true meaning. There are two possible ways to understand the term. In its original and oldest sense, *carpe diem* as used by the Roman poet Horace was intended to mean "enjoy this present moment" in view of the brevity of life. This line of understanding persisted for a long time until another one started. The seventeenth-century poet Robert Herrick used the idea of *carpe diem* to mean "seize the day" because no one's life is uncertain. In recent years the latter meaning of *carpe diem* has become the dominant way of understanding the term, especially after the 1989 movie *Dead Poets Society* popularized it. The

along the lines of the seventh and eighth days of creation, then *carpe diem* is the right response.

The Christian Meaning of Carpe Diem

While it is fashionable today to use the watchword *carpe diem* as a philosophy of life, the Bible warns us how to properly "seize the day." There is a right way and a wrong way of doing so. Thus, we must pursue a Christian approach to *carpe diem.*

Carpe Diem—Deo Volente

In James 4:13–17, the apostle James admonishes those who are confident about "seizing the day":

> Come now, you who say, "Today or tomorrow we will go to such and such a city, and spend a year there and engage in business and make a profit." Yet you do not know what your life will be like tomorrow. You are just a vapor that appears for a little while and then vanishes away. Instead, you ought to say, "If the Lord wills, we will live and also do this or that." But as it is, you boast in your arrogance; all such boasting is evil. Therefore, to one who knows the right thing to do and does not do it, to him it is sin.

Despite God's promised provision, James's instruction is closer to the idea of merely enjoying this present moment that God has given us because that is really the only sure thing one has. Thus, his counsel is to proceed with the attitude of *Deo volente* ("if the Lord wills").

The church has taken James's admonition so seriously that, through the years, there was even a practice among Christians to always attach the letters *D. V.* (standing for *Deo volente*) to their stated plans. Others, though, would write down *Deo volente, carpe diem.* Such a combination is consistent with the spirit of James 4, for the apostle James is not opposed to planning or active living; rather, it is the lack of giving consideration to God's providence that he is rebuking.

---

older sense seems to call for a more relaxed approach to life, whereas the newer sense seems to call for a more aggressive approach to all the opportunities that life has to offer.

Carpe Diem—Coram Deo

There is also another biblical approach that corresponds to *carpe diem*. It is found in what the psalmist says in Psalm 16:7–11:

> [7] I will bless the Lord who has counseled me;
> Indeed, my mind instructs me in the night.
> [8] I have set the Lord continually before me;
> Because He is at my right hand, I will not be shaken.
> [9] Therefore my heart is glad and my glory rejoices;
> My flesh also will dwell securely.
> [10] For You will not abandon my soul to Sheol;
> Nor will You allow Your Holy One to undergo decay.
> [11] You will make known to me the path of life;
> In Your presence is fullness of joy;
> In Your right hand there are pleasures forever.

Note in verse 8 how confident the psalmist is about what lies ahead of him. He is truly living *carpe diem*. And yet this confident attitude is tempered by what he says he did before embracing it. He exhibited *coram Deo* ("living before the face of the Lord"). He says, "I have set the Lord continually before me" (v. 8). That is the basis for his confident living. Can we live *carpe diem* in the sense of "seize the day"? Yes, provided, of course, we practice *coram Deo*. Thus, when we live *coram Deo*, we can live *carpe diem*.

Carpe Diem and the Seventh and Eighth Days of Creation

The brief biblical discussion above shows that *carpe diem* has to be lived out with care for and attention toward God. "Seize the day" does not mean doing so with no regard for God in such an endeavor. As John Webster says of this kind of lifestyle, "Creaturely self-government is destructive and enslaving, because it exchanges the divine necessity for some other self-imposed necessity, less wise and loving than that appointed by God, and leading not to our happiness but to decay."[45]

Who, then, can truly live the life of *carpe diem*? It is the person who not only knows God's providence of the seventh day of creation but also

45. Webster, *God without Measure*, 141.

has entered the eighth day of creation in Christ. The long form of the watchword would be *carpe diem, inhabitare dies octavus* ("inhabit the eighth day"). For it is the person who has entered into the eighth day of creation and operates from within that frame of mind who will naturally live out the correct *carpe diem*.

A World Awaiting the Master's Masterpiece

The world is full of Bill Murrays who have come to the end of themselves. They desperately need hope. God's wonderful doctrine of providence is the masterpiece that can speak deeply to their soul and change their life for the better. But, unfortunately, many times the masterpiece is not properly placed in the museum gallery. It is not framed properly to benefit those around it. Thus, this chapter—indeed, the entire book—has suggested that the masterpiece of the doctrine of providence needs reframing.

The new frame fitted for the masterpiece is the motif of the seventh and eighth days of creation. This theological frame's four sides consist of the dramatic side, the existential side, the boundary-setting side, and

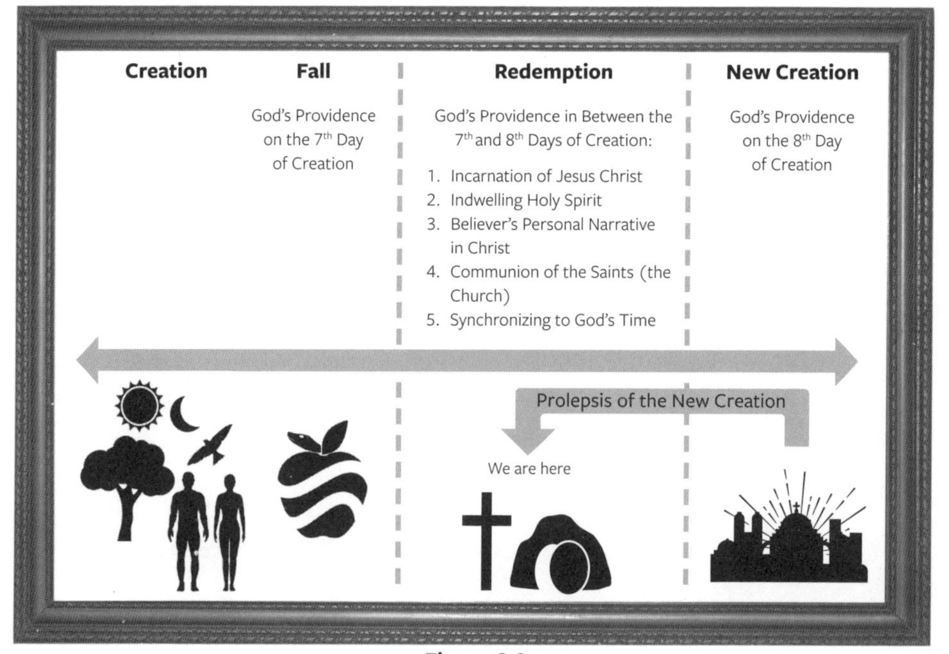

Figure 8.2

the invitational side. It is hoped that just as *The Song of the Lark* at the Art Institute of Chicago was able to save Bill Murray, God's masterpiece of the doctrine of providence will do the same for many lives who come to encounter it along with its four-sided theological frame.

But if the masterpiece is to have its desired impact on lives, then, unlike *The Song of the Lark*, it must not just be hung in the museum's gallery. Rather, it must be prominently placed in the musings of the gallery of the human mind, capturing the heart's imagination. This book seeks to reframe the doctrine of God's providence—within the framework of God's seventh and eighth days of creation—as something to be not merely ruminated on or debated but inhabited.

Bibliography

Anderson, Ray S. *On Being Human: Essays in Theological Anthropology*. Grand Rapids: Eerdmans, 1982.

Augustine. *Sermons 94A–147A*. Edited by John E. Rotelle. Translation and notes by Edmund Hill. The Works of St. Augustine III/4. New York: New City, 1992.

Barth, Karl. *Church Dogmatics* III/3. Edited by G. W. Bromiley and T. F. Torrance. Edinburgh: T&T Clark, 1960.

———. *Prayer*. Edited by Don E. Saliers. Translated by Sara F. Terrien. 2nd ed. Philadelphia: Westminster, 1985.

Berkouwer, G. C. *The Providence of God*. Translated by Lewis B. Smedes. Grand Rapids: Eerdmans, 1952.

Blowers, Paul M. *Drama of the Divine Economy: Creator and Creation in Early Christian Theology and Piety*. Oxford: Oxford University Press, 2012.

Bonhoeffer, Dietrich. *The Cost of Discipleship*. New York: Touchstone, 1959.

———. *Ethics*. Edited by Eberhard Bethge. New York: Macmillan, 1955.

Boyd, Gregory A. *Satan and the Problem of Evil: Constructing a Trinitarian Warfare Theodicy*. Downers Grove, IL: InterVarsity, 2001.

Braaten, Carl E. *Christ and the Counter-Christ: Apocalyptic Themes in Theology and Culture*. Philadelphia: Fortress, 1972.

Brunner, Emil. *The Christian Doctrine of God*. Translated by Olive Wyon. Philadelphia: Westminster, 1950.

———. *The Theology of Crisis*. New York: Scribner's Sons, 1931

Calvin, John. *Institutes of the Christian Religion*. Edited by John T. McNeill. Translated by Ford Lewis Battles. 2 vols. Philadelphia: Westminster, 1960.

Carson, D. A. *Divine Sovereignty and Human Responsibility: Biblical Perspectives in Tension*. Eugene, OR: Wipf & Stock, 2002.

———. *From the Resurrection to His Return: Living Faithfully in the Last Days*. Fearn, Scotland: Christian Focus, 2010.

Chesterton, G. K. *Orthodoxy*. San Francisco: Ignatius, 1995.

———. *What I Saw in America*. London: Hodder & Stoughton, 1922.

Cottrell, Jack. "The Nature of Divine Sovereignty." In *The Grace of God and the Will of Man*, edited by Clark H. Pinnock, 97–119. Minneapolis: Bethany House, 1989.

Cox, Harvey. *The Secular City: A Celebration of Its Liberties and an Invitation to Its Discipline*. New York: Macmillan, 1965.

Crichton-Miller, Emma. "What Goes Around: The Art of Framing." Christie's, April 29, 2015. https://www.christies.com/features/Frames-in-Focus-5815-1.aspx.

Culver, Robert Duncan. *The Living God*. Wheaton: Victor, 1978.

Daane, James. "Creating a Respect for Theology." *Christian Century* 94, February 2–9, 1977, 89–90.

Eichrodt, Walther. *Theology of the Old Testament*. Translated by J. A. Baker. 2 vols. Philadelphia: Westminster, 1961.

Fairweather, Eugene R. *The Meaning and Message of Lent: How an Understanding of Lent Can Deepen the Life of the Church and of the Individual Christian*. New York: Harper & Brothers, 1962.

Feinberg, John S. "God Ordains All Things." In *Predestination and Free Will: Four Views of Divine Sovereignty and Human Freedom*, edited by David Basinger and Randall Basinger, 19–43. Downers Grove, IL: InterVarsity, 1986.

González, Justo. "John Calvin, Theologian in Exile." *Apuntes* 37, no. 3 (2017): 108–21.

Gorringe, T. J. *God's Theatre: A Theology of Providence*. London: SCM, 1991.

Grenz, Stanley. *Reason for Hope: The Systematic Theology of Wolfhart Pannenberg*. 2nd ed. Grand Rapids: Eerdmans, 2005.

Grudem, Wayne. *Systematic Theology: An Introduction to Biblical Doctrine*. Grand Rapids: Zondervan, 1994.

Gunton, Colin. *The Christian Faith: An Introduction to Christian Doctrine*. Oxford: Blackwell, 2002.

Heifetz, Ronald, Alexander Grashow, and Marty Linsky. *The Practice of Adaptive Leadership: Tools and Tactics for Changing Your Organization and the World*. Boston: Harvard Business Press, 2009.

Helm, Paul. *The Providence of God*. Downers Grove, IL: InterVarsity, 1994.

Hesselink, I. John. "Calvin's Theology." In *The Cambridge Companion to John Calvin*, edited by Donald K. McKim. Cambridge: Cambridge University Press, 2004.

Hodge, A. A. *Evangelical Theology*. London: Thomas Nelson, 1890.

———. *Outlines in Theology*. New York: Armstrong and Sons, 1908.

Hodge, Charles. *Systematic Theology*. 3 vols. New York: Charles Scribner, 1872.

Horton, Michael. *The Christian Faith: A Systematic Theology for Pilgrims on the Way*. Grand Rapids: Zondervan, 2011.

House, Paul. "The Day of the Lord." In *Central Themes in Biblical Theology: Mapping Unity in Diversity*, edited by Scott J. Hafemann and Paul R. House, 179–224. Grand Rapids: Baker Academic, 2007.

Irenaeus of Lyons. *Against Heresies*. In *The Ante-Nicene Fathers: Translations of the Writings of the Fathers down to A.D. 325*, edited by Alexander Roberts and James Donaldson, vol. 1. New York: Christian Literature, 1885–1887. Reprint, Peabody, MA: Hendrickson, 1994.

Isaacson, Walter. *Steve Jobs*. New York: Simon & Schuster, 2011.

Kant, Immanuel. *Critique of Pure Reason*. Translated by Paul Guyer and Allen W. Wood. Cambridge: Cambridge University Press, 1998.

Ladd, George Eldon. *The Presence of the Future: The Eschatology of Biblical Realism*. Rev. ed. Grand Rapids: Eerdmans, 2002.

Lewis, C. S. *Mere Christianity*. New York: HarperCollins, 1952.

Lewis, Gordon, and Bruce Demarest. *Integrative Theology*. Vol. 2. Grand Rapids: Zondervan, 1990.

Lloyd-Jones, D. Martyn. *Great Doctrines of the Bible*. Wheaton: Crossway, 2003.

Löwith, Karl. *Meaning in History: The Theological Implications of the Philosophy of History*. Chicago: University of Chicago Press, 1949.

Luther, Martin. "Exposition of Psalm 147." In *Luther's Works*, vol. 14, *Selected Psalms III*, edited by Jaroslav Pelikan, 107–36. St. Louis: Concordia, 1955.

———. *Lectures on Romans*. Translated and edited by Wilhelm Pauck. Philadelphia: Westminster, 1961.

Macaskill, Grant. *Living in Union with Christ: Paul's Gospel and Christian Moral Identity*. Grand Rapids: Baker Academic, 2019.

MacIntyre, Alasdair. *After Virtue: A Study in Moral Theory*. 3rd ed. Notre Dame, IN: University of Notre Dame Press, 2007.

Marcus Aurelius. *Meditations*. Translated by Martin Hammond. New York: Penguin, 2006.

McGee, J. Vernon. *Esther: The Romance of Providence*. Nashville: Nelson, 1982.

McGrath, Alister. "Hesitations about Special Divine Action: Reflections on Some Scientific, Cultural and Theological Concerns." *European Journal for Philosophy of Religion* 7, no. 4 (2015): 3–22.

Middleton, J. Richard. *A New Heaven and a New Earth: Reclaiming Biblical Eschatology*. Grand Rapids: Baker Academic, 2013.

Muggeridge, Malcolm. *A Third Testament: A Modern Pilgrim Explores the Spiritual Wanderings of Augustine, Blake, Pascal, Tolstoy, Bonhoeffer, Kierkegaard, and Dostoevsky*. Farmington, PA: Plough, 2007.

Murray, John. "Common Grace." *Westminster Seminary Journal* 5 (November 1942): 1–28.

Niebuhr, Reinhold. *The Nature and Destiny of Man: A Christian Interpretation*. Vol. 2, *Human Destiny*. New York: Scribner's Sons, 1964.

Olson, Roger E. *Against Calvinism*. Grand Rapids: Zondervan, 2011.

———. *Arminianism FAQ: Everything You Always Wanted to Know*. Franklin, TN: Seedbed, 2024.

———. *The Mosaic of Christian Belief: Twenty Centuries of Unity and Diversity*. Downers Grove, IL: InterVarsity, 2002.

Oord, Thomas Jay. *The Uncontrolling Love of God: An Open and Relational Account of Providence*. Downers Grove, IL: InterVarsity, 2015.

Oswalt, John. "Rest." In *New International Dictionary of Old Testament Theology and Exegesis*, edited by Willem A. VanGemeren, 4:1132–36. Grand Rapids: Zondervan, 1997.

Packer, J. I. *Knowing God*. Downers Grove, IL: InterVarsity, 1973.

Pannenberg, Wolfhart. *Theology and the Kingdom of God*. Philadelphia: Westminster, 1969.

Peters, Ted. *God—The World's Future: Systematic Theology for a New Era*. 2nd ed. Minneapolis: Fortress, 2000.

Phares, Ross. *Bible in Pocket, Gun in Hand: The Story of Frontier Religion*. Lincoln: University of Nebraska Press, 1964.

Pink, Daniel H. *Drive: The Surprising Truth about What Motivates Us*. New York: Riverhead, 2009.

Pinnock, Clark H. "From Augustine to Arminius: A Pilgrimage in Theology." In *The Grace of God and the Will of Man*, edited by Clark H. Pinnock, 15–30. Minneapolis: Bethany House, 1989.

Piper, John. *What Is Saving Faith? Reflections on Receiving Christ as a Treasure*. Wheaton: Crossway, 2022.

Reno, R. R. *Redemptive Change: Atonement and the Christian Cure of the Soul*. Harrisburg, PA: Trinity Press International, 2002.

Rice, Richard. "Divine Foreknowledge and Free-Will Theism." In *The Grace of God and the Will of Man*, edited by Clark H. Pinnock, 121–39. Minneapolis: Bethany House, 1989.

Rule, Andrew K. "Providence and Preservation." In *Basic Christian Doctrines*, edited by Carl F. H. Henry. New York: Holt, Rhinehart and Winston, 1962.

Sandel, Michael J. *The Tyranny of Merit: What's Become of the Common Good?* New York: Farrar, Straus and Giroux, 2020.

Schmemann, Alexander. "Liturgy and Eschatology." *Sobornost* 7 (1985): 6–14.

Smith, James K. A. *How (Not) to Be Secular: Reading Charles Taylor*. Grand Rapids: Eerdmans, 2014.

Stott, John R. W. *Basic Christianity*. Downers Grove, IL: InterVarsity, 1971.

———. *Through the Bible, Through the Year: Daily Reflections from Genesis to Revelation*. Grand Rapids: Baker Books, 2006.

Swinton, John. *Raging with Compassion: Pastoral Responses to the Problem of Evil*. Grand Rapids: Eerdmans, 2007.

Taylor, Charles. *A Secular Age*. Cambridge, MA: Belknap Press of Harvard University Press, 2007.

Thomas Aquinas. *Summa theologica*. Translated by Fathers of the English Dominican Province. 3 vols. New York: Benziger, 1947–48.

Tilley, Terrence W. *The Evils of Theodicy*. Eugene, OR: Wipf & Stock, 2000.

Vanhoozer, Kevin J. *The Drama of Doctrine: A Canonical-Linguistic Approach to Christian Theology*. Louisville: Westminster John Knox, 2005.

———. *Remythologizing Theology: Divine Action, Passion and Authorship*. Cambridge: Cambridge University Press, 2010.

von Rad, Gerhard. *Genesis: A Commentary*. Translated by John H. Marks. Philadelphia: Westminster, 1972.

Vos, Wiebe, and Geoffrey Wainright, eds. *Liturgical Time: Papers Read at the 1981 Congress of Societas Liturgica*. Rotterdam: Liturgical Ecumenical Center Trust, 1982.

Walton, John. *Genesis*. Grand Rapids: Zondervan, 2001.

Warren, Rick. *The Purpose-Driven Life*. Grand Rapids: Zondervan, 2002.

Webster, John. *God without Measure: Working Papers in Christian Theology*. Vol. 1, *God and the Works of God*. London: Bloomsbury T&T Clark, 2016.

Williams, Pat. *How to Be like Walt: Capturing the Disney Magic Every Day of Your Life*. Deerfield Beach, FL: Health Communications, 2004.

Wright, N. T. *Surprised by Hope: Rethinking Heaven, the Resurrection, and the Mission of the Church*. New York: HarperOne, 2008.

Scripture Index

Subject Index